A Garland of Immortal Wish-fulfilling Trees

ཀ༔གཞན་བརྒྱ་ཕི་བདུན་ཏ་ཤ་ཡ་སྐ་སྐ་ཤ་ཀྱི་ཁྱི་ཁྱབ་ཐབ་ཐ་ཆིཆ་དྐ་བ་ཁྲི་ད་རཙི་སྐ།   ✠

ཞེམ་མ་ར་རོ་ཱ་ཱི་རི་ཱ་ཧུ༔ ཿ ཀྱ་མ་ལ་ཝ་ཤྲེ་ཡེ་ཱུ་ཥི་བི་ར་ཡ་ཟ་ན་རྀ་ད་ཀྱཱི་ཉ་བི་ད་ར་ད་ཥུ།   ‖

རྒྱ་ལ་དབང་དད་བལ་སྤྱལ་བའི་ གད་རབས་བརྩེ་ནཱ་ཱ་ཆི་ནད་ ད་ཊ་ས་འདུའི་སྐྱིན་བའི་སྒྲོན་བའི་བཞི་ས་རུབ་འཁྱུབ་བ་ཤྟུགས་སྐ།   ༈

THE ASTONISHING SUCCESSION OF THRONE HOLDERS
OF THE VICTORIOUS AND POWERFUL
PALYUL TRADITION CALLED

A Garland of Immortal Wish-fulfilling Trees

The Palyul Tradition of the Nyingmapas

The Venerable Tsering Lama Jampal Zangpo

TRANSLATED BY
Sangye Khandro

SNOW LION

Snow Lion
An imprint of Shambhala Publications, Inc.
2129 13th Street
Boulder, Colorado 80302
www.shambhala.com

© 1988 Pacific Yeshe Nyingpo
This edition published 2024

Cover art: Robert Beer

9 8 7 6 5 4 3 2 1

Printed in the United States of America

Shambhala Publications makes every effort
to print on acid-free, recycled paper.
Snow Lion is distributed worldwide by
Penguin Random House, Inc., and its subsidiaries.

THE LIBRARY OF CONGRESS CATALOGUES THE
PREVIOUS EDITION OF THIS BOOK AS FOLLOWS:

Names: Tshe-riṅ Bla-ma 'Jam-dpal-bzaṅ-po, Rmugs-saṅs,
1900 or 1901–, author. | Khandro, Sangye, translator.
Title: The astonishing succession of throne holders of the victorious and
powerful Palyul tradition called A garland of immortal wish-fulfilling trees /
by Tsering Lama Jampal Zangpo; translated by Sangye Khandro.
Other titles: Rgyal dbaṅ dpal yul ba'i gdan rabs ṅo mtshar 'chi med yoṅs
'du'i ljon pa'i phreṅ ba źes bya ba bźugs so. English
Related titles: Garland of immortal wish-fulfilling trees
Description: 1st ed. | Ithaca, N.Y., U.S.A.: Snow Lion Publications, 1988.
Identifiers: LCCN 88019481 | ISBN 9781645473565 (pbk.: 2024 ed.) |
ISBN 9780937938645 (pbk.: 1988 ed.)
Subjects: LCSH: Rnying-ma-pa lamas—China—
Tibet Autonomous Region—Biography.
Classification: LCC BQ7662.9.A2 J3613 1988 | DDC 294.3/923/0922 B 19
LC record available at https://lccn.loc.gov/88019481

This book is dedicated to the memory of the Venerable Second Dzongnang Rinpoche, Jampal Lodrö who lived his life in the service of the Nyingmapa Palyul tradition and who will be remembered and cherished as a great bodhisattva of this century. May his swift rebirth join us to carry on his enlightened activity!

Contents

An Introduction to the Palyul Tradition
by the Third Drubwang Pedma Norbu Rinpoche

In the snow land of Tibet, six great mother monasteries uphold the doctrine of the Great Secret Nyingmapa. In the East, the principal monastery of these six is the glorious and powerful Palyul. This book, *A Garland of Immortal Wish-Fulfilling Trees*, presents a comprehensive explanation of the extraordinary Palyul tradition. Within this tradition, the Non-dual Great Seal *Mahamudra*-Great Perfection *Ati Yoga* and the *kama* and *terma* lineages are joined together as one great river of practice.

From the time of the primordial protector, *Samantabhadra*, down to our own root gurus, the Palyul tradition has hosted hundreds and thousands of beings who have achieved the rainbow body and other profound accomplishments.

The Palyul monastery was originally the seat of the great lama, Kye-rei Chökyong Wangpo. The land the monastery is situated upon was blessed by the presence of many great bodhisattvas, dating back to the time of the three great dharma kings. Countless realized *siddhas* have visited this place and there are many accounts of these yogis flying through space between Kathog and Mugsang to propagate and receive dharma teachings.

In accordance with the ripening of past prayers, the great Vidyadhara Kunzang Sherab later came to stay at the monastery. It was at this time that the Palyul tradition was established and the monastery named Palyul Namgyal Changchub Chöling became one of the major Nyingmapa monastic institutions.

From that time until my present incarnation as the eleventh throne holder of the Palyul tradition, many troubled times have passed. However, due to the strength of the profound prayers made by many realized beings of the past, this stainless lineage has been maintained in an unbroken line to the present day. The original, undefiled blessings have been kept in not only the mother monastery, but also in the thousands of branch monasteries. These monasteries housed nearly 100,000 members of the sangha who persevered in scholastic and meditative accomplishment, as well as the culmination of enlightened activity.

At this particular time in the world, the conditions are especially ripe for the practice of this tradition of the unceasing dharma nectar of the Non-dual Great Seal *Mahamudra-Great Perfection Ati Yoga* and the lineages of *kama* and *terma*. Towards this pursuit, I persevere both day and night, with the intention of benefiting the Buddhist doctrine in general and, specifically, our own Palyul tradition, which is like my eyes and heart, so that the doctrine of the precious oral transmission lineage of the profound *Ati Yoga* will never diminish.

In order to satisfy the interest of fortunate, faithful aspirants, and as an offering to the precious holders of the lineage, I requested the vajra-holder, Gelong Tsering Lama, who is also known as Jampal Zangpo, to write this *Garland of Immortal Wish-Fulfilling Trees*. In addition, I have observed the common wishes and needs of the knowledgeable and impartial people of the western world, who are following the great teachers of the past by internalizing the essential instructions to accomplish the non-dual state of Vajradharahood in one body and in one lifetime. In order to fulfill their needs, and in accordance with my aspirations, this text was translated into the English language by Sangye Khandro and others, without any hesitation or concern for personal hardships.

I, Palyul Pedma Norbu, the eleventh Throne Holder of the Palyul tradition, have written this in the western year of 1986, with the prayer that the virtue accumulated by the production of this book may increase and propagate the sacred doctrine of the three inner *yogas*, so they may encompass this earth and remain firm indefinitely! May excellent, supreme virtue prevail!

The Venerable Tsering Lama Jampal Zangpo

Tsering Lama was born in the Mugsang Pedra village of Dege, into the Langchung family heritage known for producing a strong line of excellent scholars and practitioners. As a youth, Tsering Lama took ordination and stayed at Mugsang monastery, studying reading and writing and performing *sadhana* (means of accomplishment) practice. He learned all the important subjects without difficulty.

Tsering Lama later traveled to the mother Palyul monastery and received many profound transmissions from the great Khenpo Ngaga Rinpoche, the second Drubwang Pedma Norbu Rinpoche, the fourth Karma Kuchen Rinpoche, the second Chögtrul Rinpoche and many other precious lamas. These transmissions included the *Nyingma Kama*, the *Rinchen Ter Dzöd* (Precious Terma Treasury), the *Nam Chö* revelations, Ratna Lingpa's revelations, *Kagyed* (Eight Herukas), *Gongdu* (Condensed Enlightened Mind) and essentially all the empowerments, transmissions and commentaries practiced in the Palyul tradition.

Although all of Tsering Lama's teachers loved and cared for him as though he was their own son, his principal, extraordinary root guru was the omniscient second Drubwang Pedma Norbu Rinpoche, with whom he remained for many years. It was due to his root guru's kindness that Tsering Lama became learned in each of the major sciences, including Sanskrit, grammar, logic, poetry, composition and astrology. He made a thorough study of all the important *tantras* such as the *Yönten Dzöd* (Treasury of Pure Qualities), *Yidshin Dzöd* (Wish-Fulfilling Treasury), the *Gyud Sangwai Nyingpo* (Secret Essence) and others. Achieving understanding and realization through his studies, Tsering Lama became well-known as a truly qualified scholar.

He later entered the traditional three year retreat at the Palyul Retreat Center, completing all the recitation accomplishments of the Three Roots, the five hundred thousand accumulations of the preliminary practices, *tsa-lung*, *trekchöd* and *tögyal*. Having successfully completed all of the stages of inner practice, Tsering Lama received the title of *Vajra Acharya* (tantric master).

It was at this point in his life that Tsering Lama had the great good fortune to teach writing, poetry, astrology, grammar and other subjects to the third Drubwang Pedma Norbu Rinpoche, the reincarnation of his root guru, and to the second Dzongnang Rinpoche, Tulku Thubten Palzang, as well as many high-ranking government officials of Dege. Tsering Lama was blessed in having met four of the throne holders of the Palyul lineage from whom he heard the stories of their lives and the activities of their predecessors. His direct experience greatly enhances the authenticity of these accounts. In addition to this book, Tsering Lama composed a large volume of poetic praise in honor of the most important gurus of the Nyingmapa tradition. Tsering Lama selflessly served the Palyul lineage with every thought, word and action until, at the age of eighty-four, he passed into the sphere of truth.

This brief biography of Tsering Lama was written by Khenpo Namdrol of Palyul Namdroling Monastery, in South India.

Translator's Note

In 1985 the third Drubwang Pedma Norbu Rinpoche made his first visit to the West and Far East. His Holiness had contacted the Venerable Gyatrul Rinpoche asking for his assistance in the coordination of his schedule to visit the United States, and it was at that time that Gyatrul Rinpoche requested that His Holiness give the profound and rare *Nam Chö* (Space Treasure) empowerments at Tashi Chöling (Dharma Place of Good Fortune), which is the retreat center for Pacific Yeshe Nyingpo, located in southern Oregon.

As the preparations progressed, it was apparent that western students knew little of His Holiness or of the Palyul tradition, but as Gyatrul Rinpoche began answering our questions, we became more aware of the significance of this great *Bodhisattva*. I had the good fortune and honor of being able to make the oral translations from Tibetan into English for His Holiness during the *Nam Chö* empowerments and I felt a deep connection developing between us.

At the invitation of His Holiness, Gyatrul Rinpoche journeyed to South India in January of 1986 to participate in the important ceremonies surrounding the Tibetan New Year *(Losar)*, and I was able to accompany him on the trip. I had, during my fourteen years as a student of Tibetan Buddhism, made many pilgrimages to India and Nepal, studying with teachers living in the Himalayan foothills, but this was my first opportunity to travel to South India and the first time I had ever experienced such strong activity and vitality at a traditional monastic center of learning and accomplishment.

Namdroling monastery, which was built by Pedma Norbu Rinpoche and is supported solely by his efforts, is an extraordinary training center. The young *tulkus* of the Palyul tradition are personally supervised by His Holiness and he oversees and guides the monastery's scholastic college, which presently has over one hundred students, making it the largest Nyingma college in the world. He is personally involved in the teaching of those practitioners who are undertaking the three year retreat and he presides over all the regular major and minor ceremonies performed by the five hundred monks in residence at the monastery. He cares for the spiritual and many physical needs of the surrounding community of ten thousand Tibetan laypeople.

Because of His Holiness' great kindness, I was fortunate to receive many teachings and transmissions that had never been received before by a woman. As my stay progressed at Namdroling monastery, I realized more and more the great importance of the Palyul tradition, not only in the present day, but even more significantly, how deeply entwined it was in the entire history of Buddhism in Tibet.

Toward the end of our visit, Khenpo Namdrol, a highly qualified teacher in the Scholastic College, brought to me the precious text of the history of the Palyul tradition, asking if I would translate it into English. This text had been written, at Pedma Norbu Rinpoche's request, by one of the senior lamas who was still in Tibet. It was at the request of His Holiness and with the urging and support of Khenpo Namdrol and his brother, Kunzang Lama, that I began the translation the very next day.

For the next month and a half I worked closely with Khenpo Namdrol and Ngawang Paljor, an English-speaking attendant of His Holiness, going through the entire text while listening to Khenpo's commentary and patient explanation. By the time we left India, the first rough draft of *A Garland of Immortal Wish-fulfilling Trees* had been completed. To Khenpo Namdrol and Ngawang Paljor I give sincere thanks for their gracious assistance with the actual translation.

In the months since returning, others have given their assistance. I would like to acknowledge and thank Jane Gamble Hall and Mitchell Frangadakis for their help in preparing the text. I would like to thank Ani Sonam Paldron for all her assistance with text preparation, format, editing and publication research, and Jeanne Elliott for her grammatical editorial assistance. Special thanks go to the Sangha of Tulku Ahkön Norbu Lhamo at Kunzang Odsal Palyul Changchub Chöling, whose technical and professional assistance was indispensable.

Finally, and most especially, I wish to express my thanks to the

Venerable Gyatrul Rinpoche who assisted me with his wisdom and knowledge of the content and for his patience and unfailing humor and compassion throughout the entire experience of translating this text.

It is my sincere prayer that this translation has been made without error and that all the Buddhas and *bodhisattvas* will purify and bless this endeavor. May this tiny drop of effort merge with the great ocean of truth, merit and virtue so that sentient beings will be ultimately liberated from the endless cycle of existence and achieve the state of full-awakening. May the lives of the precious spiritual teachers be firm and long so that the glorious wheel of truth may continue to turn forever in all realms of existence.

Sangye Khandro
(Nanci Gustafson)
Tashi Chöling
November, 1986

Author's Prayer

In the originally pure, great victorious state
of pure-awareness, full-awakening is actualized
as the six specific dharmas.[1]

The astonishing display of countless pure realms and enlightened bodies
is the spontaneously accomplished, brilliantly clear, unobstructed multitude of
illusory manifestation as all-pervasive as space.

May the illuminating and glorious life story of
the victorious lotus-born guru, Padmasambhava, adorn my mind.

The three inner yogas of the generation class of **Maha Yoga,**
  the transmission class of **Anu Yoga**
  and the mind, expanse and essential instruction classes
  of **Ati Yoga** *are chariots², pulling the powerful sun*
  to clarify the doctrine of the Lord Buddha.
To those beings who uphold the doctrine
  of the great secret vehicle of Nyingmapa,
  I bow down in reverence.

In the glorious fully endowed land of Tibet,
  the Buddha's doctrine of teaching and practice
  is absolutely victorious in all directions.
I bow in reverence to the successive throne holders
  of the Palyul tradition,
  who raised the victory banner of the dharma
  of full-awakening in this world.

The Glorious Absolutely Victorious Dharma Place of Full-
Awakening *is the name of the mother Palyul monastery.*

Palyul	*Namgyal*
The Glorious Country	*Absolutely Victorious*
Chang Chub	*Chö Ling*
Full-Awakening	*Dharma Place*

Palyul Namgyal Chang Chub Chö Ling

This great secret vehicle of Nyingmapa
Is a wish-fulfilling lasso
Of the six great qualities³
Of the great secret clear light.
At the feet of the founding father, Kunzang Sherab,
Who pulls fortunate beings to the realm of original purity,
I bow down.

The light rays of the nine characteristics[4]
Of scholarship and accomplishment
Enhance and nourish the lotus forest of Buddha's doctrine.
May the lotus feet of the morning sun,
The second Drubwang Pedma Norbu,
Remain constantly implanted in the lotus of my heart.
In this, the great dharma ocean of teaching and practice,
The naga king and his assembly
Enjoy the accomplishment of scholarship and realization.
In order to reveal just how these accomplishments are achieved.

A Garland of Immortal Wish-Fulfilling Trees
Has been written.

Introduction

Originally in India, the land of Aryas, there was no distinction between the earlier and later schools of Buddhism. However, in Tibet, the land of snow mountain ranges, this distinction exists and different paths have emerged. Unless one enters the path that leads to liberation, there is no way to achieve the ultimate goal. The secret mantra clear light Great Perfection school of the Nyingmapa upholds the doctrinal principles and practices which accomplish the ultimate goal.

The six major mother monasteries upholding the doctrinal principles of the Nyingmapa school are likened to Lake Manasarowara,[5] the source of all Asian rivers. These monasteries are: Dorje Drag and Mindroling, located in the upper province of Tibet; Shechen and Dzogchen, located in the central province; and Kathog and Palyul, located in the lower province. Like the reverberating beat of a great drum, the fame of these six monasteries resounds through the three worlds.[6]

This treatise on the succession of throne holders of the victorious and powerful Palyul monastery and tradition, will reveal the source of the dharma lineages in the Palyul tradition and the succession of throne holders of the Palyul tradition and monastery. The first section of the treatise has three divisions: the source of the long lineage of *kama*; the source of the short lineage of *terma* and the source of the profound lineage of pure vision.

सरोरुहवज्र

Guru Rinpoche. (Drawing by Namkhah Tashi.)

1 The Source of the Dharma Lineages in the Palyul Tradition

1. THE LONG LINEAGE OF *KAMA*

In the Nyingmapa school, the generation class of *Maha Yoga*, transmission class *Anu Yoga* and the Great Perfection classes of *Ati Yoga* are well-known as the extraordinary vehicles. Each of these three yogas has two general classes, which are the class of *tantra* and the class of accomplishment. In the class of *tantra* of generation *Maha Yoga*, there are eight categories,[1] which include the root *Maha Yoga Tantra, Sangwai Nyingpo* (Secret Essence). In the class of *tantra* of transmission *Anu Yoga*, there are four categories,[2] which include the root *Anu Yoga Tantra, Gongpa Dupa* (Condensed Essence of the Enlightened Mind). In Great Perfection *Ati Yoga* there are three categories: the mind class, the expanse class, and the essential instruction class. The mind class is comprised of five earlier and thirteen later translations.[3] The expanse class is comprised of the *Dorje Zam-pa* (Vajra Bridge) and the essential instruction class is comprised of seventeen *tantras*.[4]

Each of the transmissions of these three inner yogas mingled together, as one great river, to become the complete oral tradition of Panchen Vimalamitra, Lotsawa Berotsana, and Acharya Padmasambhava. This tradition was transmitted in succession to the omniscient Zurchen Shakya Jungney, to Zurchung Sherab Dragpa and to Sangdag Shakya Senge. In accordance with their spiritual authorization, these masters lived their lives solely for the benefit of others, engaging in miraculous activities that were equal to boundless space. In Tibet, it was Sangdag Shakya Senge who first gave transmissions of the root *Maha Yoga Tantra, Sangwai Nyingpo* (Secret Essence). Sangdag Shakya Senge's disciple was the Dzogchen yogi, Drowai Gonpo, who was born in Domed Kampo

Gangrar. The lord of dharma, Dampa Desheg Rinpoche, (an emanation of *Manjusri*), received from Drowai Gonpo all these *Maha, Anu* and *Ati Yoga* transmissions. In addition, the fifth Dalai Lama said that Dampa Desheg Rinpoche received these transmissions directly from Shakya Senge. Both transmissions were passed from Dampa Desheg Rinpoche to the dharma lord Tsangtön Dorje Gyaltsen, to Jampa Bum and others. During this time, the one year *Anu Yoga* accomplishment, the six month *Yangdag (Sang Buddha Sama Yoga)* accomplishment, and others were performed regularly, and the *Anu* and *Ati Yogas* increased in Tibet, like the rising sun.

Jampa Bum's disciple was the great Chen-nga-wa Sonam Bum, whose disciple was Ü-öd Yeshe Bum. Ü-öd Yeshe Bum met the famous masters Sakya Pandita and Drogön Chögyal Phagpa Rinpoche while they were on their way to China. During that time, Ü-öd Yeshe Bum bestowed the *Maha Yoga* empowerments upon Drogön Chögyal Phagpa Rinpoche. In addition, he gave ordination to the second Karmapa Karma Pakshi, and performed extensive miraculous activities. His spiritual successor was Changchub Pal, a *siddha* with the power to revive the dead through the strength of his realized view and enlightened activity. During Changchub Pal's lifetime, many practitioners accomplished the rainbow light body.[5] From then on, there gradually came to be some 180,000 members of the ordained sangha in Tibet who spread forth the Buddha's Doctrine.

The next succession of lineage holders were Sonam Zangpo, Kunga Bumpa, Wangchug Palwa, Lodrö Bumpa, Lodrö Senge, Changchub Senge and Changchub Gyaltsen. Changchub Gyaltsen's disciple was the great scholar and accomplished master Bubor Yeshe Gyaltsen. Bubor Yeshe Gyaltsen received from his lama, Dra-o Chö Bum, who was an accomplished scholar and meditation master, the four rivers of transmission from the Kham tradition of the three inner yogas. The first river of transmission is the blessing of empowerment and direct introduction to the mind's nature. The second river is the oral transmission lineage of essential instructions and naked, profound secret teachings. The third river is the transmission of principal scriptures, as well as commentaries, appendixes and indexes. The fourth river is the transmission of *sadhanas* (daily practices) and the accomplishment of miraculous activities, the dharma protectors and the recitation of wrathful mantras.

Lama Dra-o Chö Bum also transmitted the three inner yogas to Lama Mogtön Dorje Palzang who then composed the important empowerment text known as *Drangtsi Chu Gyun* (A Continual Flow of Nectar). Lama Mogtön Dorje Palzang then gave the transmission of this empowerment text to the great *Bodhisattva*, Darlung Dorje Namgyal. Although this empowerment text originated in central Tibet, it is well-known to be of the Kham tradition.

Then, from Bubor Yeshe Gyaltsen, the next succession of lineage holding lamas were Namkha Gyaltsen, Ahtsi Sonam Bumpa, Drodogpa Namkha Pal Kha-wa Karpo, Namkha Gyatso, Kunga Dawa, Yang Dröd Sonam Gyaltsen, Horpo Chö Wangpa and Chöd Kang Sonam Dorje. From Chöd Kang Sonam Dorje, the transmissions were passed to Hepa Chöjung, Shakya Tashi and to Rinchen Dorje. In addition, from Chöd Kang Sonam Dorje, another transmission lineage was passed to Gyalthang Tönpa Senge and Jamyang Tashi Rinchen, the nephew of Yang Dröd Sonam Gyaltsen. Jamyang Tashi Rinchen gave the transmissions to his three principal disciples, Rongtön Rinchen Dorje, Bar Khyim Sherab Gyatso and Serlo Tönpa Gyaltsen. It was from these three disciples that the founding father of the Palyul tradition, the Vidyadhara Kunzang Sherab, received the transmissions. From then on, the *Maha, Anu* and *Ati Yogas* became like great chariots of the doctrine and up to the present day the transmission lineage of ripening empowerments, liberating commentaries and transmissions of the Nyingma *Kama* have continued without interruption.

The Source of the Great Seal Mahamudra Lineage in the Palyul Tradition

There are four major schools in the Kagyud tradition, one of which is the school of Phagmo Drugpa, founded by Dorje Gyalpo. The Phagmo Drugpa is the original source of the Martzang school, one of the eight minor schools of Kagyud, founded by Marpa Sherab Yeshe Rinchen. Of the golden lineages of the Kagyud tradition,[6] the Martzang Kagyud school is famous for holding the unbroken blessing of the practice of the Great Seal *Mahamudra*.

From the founder, Marpa Sherab Yeshe Rinchen, the Martzang school lineage continued in an unbroken line to Drogón Shingön Rinpoche (Konchog Gyaltsen), who transmitted it to the famous Ngu Chökyi Dorje, an ancestor of the king of Dege. Ngu Chökyi Dorje had previously received the transmission lineage of the

Maha, Anu and *Ati Yogas* and was engaged in these practices when he received the Martzang Kagyud *Mahamudra* transmissions. During his lifetime, Ngu Chökyi Dorje meditated in caves at the white rock of Mugsang and Drodung and his practice cave is to this day known as *Nguphug* (cave of Ngu Chökyi Dorje). He passed on the *Mahamudra* transmission to the great scholar and meditator, Bubor Yeshe Gyaltsen, to the Bodhisattva Gyaltsen Senge and to Ah Do Konchog Gyaltsen. Ah Do Konchog Gyaltsen, who now held the *Mahamudra* lineage, also received from the Bodhisattva Kunga Nyima, in the area of Shang-zar Bulung, all the empowerments and teachings of Tertön Rigzin Güd Dem's revelation *Dzogchen Gongpa Zang Thal* (The Great Perfection Penetrating Enlightened Mind). After receiving these transmissions, Ah Do Konchog Gyaltsen traveled to the retreat place of Kathog Drago to see the Bodhisattva Gyaltsen Senge, who was giving a teaching. He immediately went in and offered him the *Dzogchen Gongpa Zang Thal Terma* scriptures. To his great surprise, the *Bodhisattva* acted extremely upset and threw the *Terma* scriptures down below the retreat house. The impression of the syllables on the stone where the scripture fell can still be clearly seen. When Gyaltsen Senge finished teaching, he asked that the *Terma* scriptures be retrieved and brought to him. After reading and fully comprehending the meaning of this profound *Terma*, the Bodhisattva Gyaltsen Senge requested Ah Do Konchog Gyaltsen to give to him the empowerment and teachings. The lineage of this *Terma* was then transmitted from Ah Do Konchog Gyaltsen to the excellent scholar, Horpo Shakya Gyaltsen.

In the region of Mugsang, at the isolated place of Paldro Karma Lhateng and in the extremely remote area of the white rock of Gyaltsa, Horpo Shakya Gyaltsen composed a new commentary on the *Gongpa Zang Thal Terma* (Penetrating Enlightened Mind). This marked the beginning of the lineage known as the Non-dual Great Seal *Mahamudra*-Great Perfection *Ati Yoga*. The first recipient of this new lineage was Bubor Changchub Senge. He and his disciples practiced the profound transmission of the Non-dual Great Seal *Mahamudra*-Great Perfection *Ati Yoga* in retreat at Palyul, Drag Karchu and Paldro Tagsang. They then transmitted the lineage to Bubor Trashi Gyatso, who composed a condensed practice commentary derived from Horpo Shakya Gyaltsen's extensive commentary. This later became the main *Gongpa Zang Thal* (Penetrating Enlightened Mind) commentary used for the Non-dual Great Seal

Mahamudra-Great Perfection *Ati Yoga* practice in the Palyul tradition and is presently part of the great *Rinchen Ter Dzöd* (Precious *Terma* Treasury). The lineage was then successively transmitted to
Gyaldong Tönpa Senge, who authored yet another commentary.
Gyaldong Tönpa Senge passed the transmission to his three
disciples, Drungpa Chönyid Gyatso of Palwar Rekhe monastery,
Chökyong Gyatso of Gajey, and Serlo Tönpa Gyaltsen of
Mugsang. It was from these three disciples that the founding father
of the Palyul tradition, the great Vidyadhara Kunzang Sherab,
received the transmission.

From Kunzang Sherab to the present time, the succession of
throne holders of the Palyul tradition, as well as the greater sangha
community, have maintained the lineage of Non-dual Great Seal
Mahamudra-Great Perfection *Ati Yoga* as a principal practice, which
includes clear light *togyal*, inner *togyal*,darkness practice, dream practice, training in the nature of sound and pure realms practice.[7]
After perfect understanding and meditative realization of these
practices, superior practitioners actualize the signs of accomplishment on the path. Each monk in the Palyul monastery must perform these practices; even those with inferior capabilities perform
and accomplish the basic *shiney* (peaceful abiding) practice.[8] Due to
the strong emphasis on practice, the Palyul tradition became
known as the lineage of practice.

In addition to the three lamas from whom he received this
lineage, the Vidyadhara Kunzang Sherab received from Konchog
Tashi, Rangpo Rinchen Dorje and others, the following transmis-
sions: the *Bima Nyingthig* (Vimalamitra's Heart Essence), *Khandro Ny-
ingthig* (*Dakini's* Heart Essence); *Dzöd Dun* (Seven Treasures of
Longchenpa); *Ngalso Kor Sum* (Three Cycles on Remaining in the
Natural State); *Ya Shi* (Four Works of Jigme Lingpa); *Yangti Yidshin
Norbu* (Wish-Fulfilling Jewel, Inner Teaching); Lama Dungtso
Repai's *Yangti* (Inner Teaching) and the precious root *Nyingma Gyud
Bum*. After receiving these transmissions, the Vidyadhara Kunzang
Sherab had new copies transcribed, gave further teachings and in-
creased the doctrine.

2. THE SOURCE OF THE SHORT LINEAGE OF *TERMA* IN
   PALYUL TRADITION

The Combined Lineage of Tertön Nyang and Guru Chöwang

From the accomplishment class of *tantra*, Tertön Nyang's revelation *Kagyed Desheg Dupa* (Eight *Herukas*, Condensed Essence of the *Tathagatas*) and Guru Chöwang's revelation *Kagyed Sang Dzog* (Eight *Herukas*, Secret Perfection) combined into one lineage which was transmitted to Tertön Shigpo Lingpa, who became the second authorized keeper of this dharma. He then transmitted the lineage to Pedma Gyaltsen of Sa-ngen.

At this time, in the lower region of Kham, it was very hard to find a lama holding the lineage of empowerments and transmissions of *Kagyed* (Eight *Herukas*) and *Gongdu* (Condensed Enlightened Mind). When Bubor Tashi Gyatso sent a letter to Tertön Shigpo Lingpa requesting that a lama with the power to transmit these *termas* be sent to Kham, the Tertön sent Lama Pedma Gyaltsen. It is said that when Lama Pedma Gyaltsen went to Kham, a vulture carried all the scriptures of the *Kagyed* and *Gongdu* to Kham. There he transmitted the lineage to Tagla Pedma Lödro, who transmitted it to his disciple, Gyawen Konchog Tashi. It was from Gyawen Konchog Tashi that the founding father of the Palyul tradition, the great Vidyadhara Kunzang Sherab, received these *terma* transmissions. From that time on, the revelations of *Kagyed* (Eight *Herukas*) and *Gongdu* (Condensed Enlightened Mind), including the major and minor accomplishment ceremonies, dharma medicine accomplishments, *torma* reversals, etc., have been principal practices in the Palyul tradition.

The *terma* revelations of Guru Chowang, known as *Thugchen Yang Nying Dupa* (Condensed Innermost Essence of *Avalokiteshvara*) and *Lama Sangdu* (Condensed Secret Essence of the Guru) were transmitted by the *Tertön* to the dharma keeper, Mani Rinchen, a great *mahasiddha* of the rainbow body. From Mani Rinchen, this lineage was passed in succession to the great Vidyadhara Kunzang Sherab. From Kunzang Sherab, the lineage has been transmitted down through the line of throne holders to the greater sangha community. These *termas* of Guru Chöwang have also become principal inner practices in the Palyul tradition. They include regular performances of the major and minor accomplishment ceremonies and the *Lama Sangdu* black hat lama dance, which is performed on the auspicious tenth day of the lunar calendar.

The *terma* revelation of the great Tertön Sangye Lingpa, known as *Lama Gongdu* (Condensed Enlightened Mind of the Lama) was successively transmitted by the Tertön to Cha Kyungpa Ngawang Pedma Namgyal, Pedma Gyaltsen and to the lineage of Tagla Pedma Lodrö. The great Vidyadhara Kunzang Sherab received this lineage from Palmo Sherab Gyatso.

A prophecy in this *Gongdu Terma* states that Kunzang Sherab is a lineage holder of the revelation. In the Palyul tradition, the lineage of *Lama Gongdu*, which includes the major and minor accomplishment ceremonies and *sadhanas*, is practiced without interruption. The corresponding empowerments and teachings are transmitted on a regular basis. The Palyul monastery erected a special protector shrine for the three principal protectors of *Lama Gongdu* (*Hayagriva, Shaza Karmoche* and *Tzen*).

Each year, during the regular *Lama Gongdu* accomplishment ceremony performed at the Palyul monastery, the nectar in the vase within the mandala is replenished and each year it is found that the nectar from the previous year has not evaporated. This and other auspicious signs of accomplishment caused the omniscient Kongtrul Rinpoche, Lodrö Thaye, to remark, "The Palyul tradition in unequaled in the supreme accomplishment of *Lama Gongdu*."

The Extensive Terma Lineage of Tertön Ratna Lingpa

Tertön Ratna Lingpa's revelation *Dupa Khor Sum* (Condensed Essence of the Three Cycles) was transmitted by Sonam Tashi of Gardrung, down the extensive lineage to Pedma Wangdrag, who was Karma Chagmed Rinpoche's father. Pedma Wangdrag then transmitted the revelations to the Mahasiddha Chagmed Rinpoche. Chagmed Rinpoche wrote extensive new additions to these revelations and gave the old and new transmissions directly to the authorized dharma keeper, the great Vidyadhara Kunzang Sherab.

The Short Terma Lineage of Tertön Ratna Lingpa

The great Tertön Migyur Dorje met Tertön Ratna Lingpa in a vision and received all of his *terma* revelations directly. The Vidyadhara Kunzang Sherab then received the revelations directly from Tertön Migyur Dorje, thereby establishing the short lineage of Ratna Lingpa's *Terma* in the Palyul tradition.

Each year, for one month, the three *kaya* accomplishment of Ratna Lingpa's *Thug Drub* (Mind Accomplishment)[9] is performed on a rotating basis at the Palyul monastery. In addition, the following revelations of Ratna Lingpa are annually performed without interruption: *Thugchen Sangdu* (Condensed Secret Essence of *Avalokiteshvara); Tse Drub* (Life Accomplishment); *Gur Drag Mei Kyil* (Wrathful Guru Swirling Fire); and *Phurba Yang Sang Lamed* (Extremely Secret Unsurpassed *Vajrakilaya).* An entire protector shrine is kept for *Gonpo Ma-ning (Mahakala),* the principal protector of Ratna Lingpa's revelations. It is also the saying of many great lamas that the Palyul tradition is unequaled in the consistent practice of Ratna Lingpa's *Thug Drub* (Mind Accomplishment). The succession of throne holders and sangha have maintained these *terma mandala-sadhanas* as their innermost heart practices, through which miraculous activities abound for the benefit of all beings.

Tertön Karma Lingpa's *terma* revelation of the peaceful and wrathful deities was transmitted from the dharma keeper, Garawa Namkha Gyatso, down the line of lineage holders to Hepa Chöjung. Hepa Chöjung's tradition was transmitted to Serlo Tönpa Gyaltsen, and then to the great Vidyadhara Kunzang Sherab. Tertön Karma Lingpa's extensive lineage of the peaceful and wrathful deities and commentaries on the six *bardos,* from the Dongtrug tradition, were transmitted by the Mahasiddha Chagmed Rinpoche to Kunzang Sherab. This lineage contains the root recitation and accomplishment practices performed for the dead, which are principal practices of the Palyul tradition.

Tertön Jatsön Nyingpo's six volumes of *terma* revelations were transmitted from the dharma keeper Tenpa Dargey to Lama Nyima Gyaltsen of Mugsang. Lama Nyima Gyaltsen transmitted all of these empowerments and teachings directly to the great Vidyadhara Kunzang Sherab. Among these revelations is the profound practice of Padmasambhava as *Yidam* (Meditational Deity) *Konchog Chidu* (General Condensed Essence of the Three Jewels). From the time of Kunzang Sherab until now, this practice has been an important part of the Palyul tradition.

Tertön Namkha Rinchen's *Terma* revelation, known as *Gonpo*

Tsogdag (Protector *Mahakala*) is an *Anu Yoga* protector in the Kham tradition. This lineage was transmitted to the Vidyadhara Kunzang Sherab, who constructed a new protector shrine for this practice. In addition, he instituted this aspect of *Mahakala* to be a general protector of the Nyingmapa school.

The glorious *Heruka* Tertön Longsal Nyingpo authorized Kunzang Sherab to be the dharma keeper of his *terma* revelations. He also gave Kunzang Sherab an extremely precious *terma* image of *Thugje Chenpo Yang Sang Lamed* (*Avalokiteshvara* in the Unsurpassed, Extremely Secret Aspect).

Kunzang Sherab received many other lineage transmissions which did not become principal practices of the Palyul tradition. Some of these include: *Jampal Tsedag* (*Manjusri* Owner of Life); *Trowo, Keng-Kong, Charga* (Three Wrathful Meditational Deities); *Mati Seng Dong* (Snow Lion Faced Deity of Tertön Mati's revelations) and Tertön Shigpo Lingpa's revelations.

3. THE SOURCE OF THE PROFOUND LINEAGE OF
PURE VISION IN THE PALYUL TRADITION

Prior to Kunzang Sherab's first meeting with the Mahasiddha Chagmed Rinpoche, it was prophesied by the great Tertön Migyur Dorje that Kunzang Sherab would be the dharma keeper of the *Nam Chö* Great Perfection revelations. Tertön Migyur Dorje transmitted the entire *Avalokiteshvara* cycle of the Nam Chö Great Perfection revelations to Kunzang Sherab. Later, when Chagmed Rinpoche invited Tertön Migyur Dorje to Mugsang, Kunzang Sherab accompanied him as his attendant. It was during this visit that Tertön Migyur Dorje twice gave the entire *Nam Chö* transmissions, including the transmissions of Buddha in the Palm of the Hand. From then onward, the stages of practice of Buddha in the Palm of the Hand have been the most essential practices performed in the Palyul tradition. These practices include the one month *ngundro* preliminary practice retreat, *tsa-lung tummo* (mystic heat channels and winds) and the various stages of *Dzogchen* practice.

The daily prayers and practices performed in the Palyul monastery are the *Nam Chö* revelations, which include the annual performance of the major and minor *Nam Chö* accomplishment ceremonies and pure vision lama dances.

The great Vidyadhara Kunzang Sherab received many other

transmissions from countless spiritual teachers. Some of these transmissions include: the precious *Kagyur;* the *Lam-dre* (Path and Fruition of the Sakya School); the *Chöd* of Padampa Sangye, the Khadampa tradition, Jonang's *Ku Khor Kyen Drub* (*Kalachakra* Recitation and Accomplishment); Tertön Orgyenpa's *Dorje Shi Nyen Drub* (Peaceful Vajra Recitation and Accomplishment); and countless empowerments, general discourses and personal instructions in both the earlier and later schools. In fact, it is as though there was not a single transmission that he did not receive.

Just as a snow mountain is the source of a great river, this brief explanation reveals the source of these great dharma lineages in the Palyul tradition.

2   The Mother Palyul Monastery

In the cool, high country of Tibet, which is the emanation field of the great *Bodhisattva Avalokiteshvara*, there are three provinces. The first is the upper province of Töd Nga-Ri, which has three inner regions, like lakes of dharma. The second is the central province of Ü Tzang, with four regions, like dharma water canals, and the third is the lower province of Do Kham, having six regions, like vast dharma fields.

The mother Palyul monastery is located in the lower province of Do Kham, in the region of Bubor. The dharma lord Tsangtön was known to have said, "I, the Buddhist Dorje Gyaltsen, will be reborn in the region of Bubor." He was born in Tsamdo, which is within the region of Bubor.[1]

The Palyul monastery is situated between Pang Kang Chöling monastery, the seat of the Martzang Kagyud Lama Rinchen Lingpa and other great lamas, and Drulri Dragmar Dorje Dzong monastery, built by Labtön Namkha Rinchen. Behind the Palyul monastery is the supreme sacred place known as *Lhanyen Paldzom Dorje Dradul*. Above, to the east, is the place blessed by Garab Dorje, called *Dago Odsal Lhari*. To the south is the sacred waterfall of *Chu Sangwai Drag*, a location as sacred as *Lho Trag Kharchu*, the sacred power spot of Padmasambhava. The Palyul monastery adjoins the place where the great treasure revealers, Sang-ngag Lingpa, Rinchen Lingpa and others revealed profound *termas*. To the west, the monastery is supported by the sacred practice place of Mugsang Drodul Trinley.

When the *bodhisattva* princess of China, Gyaza Kanjo, was passing through Kham on her way to central Tibet, she inserted a staff into the ground, just below the site of the present Palyul monastery. From that spot, a bodhi tree, called *changma racho*, spontaneously appeared and remains there today. There is also a cave in

this area where Lotsawa Berotsana entered into retreat before completing a journey to *Gyamo-tsawai Rong* (Gyarong). As he passed
through the site of the present Palyul monastery, he inserted his
staff into the ground and a juniper tree spontaneously appeared,
which continues to grow there today.

The Palyul monastery is built where the great Lama Kyere
Chökyong Wangpo made his spiritual seat. Kyere Chökyong
Wangpo was one of the two famous disciples of Lotsawa Ma Rinchen Chög (the other disciple was Tsugma Rinchen), both of whom
were renowned practitioners of *Maha Yoga*. Even today, pilgrims,
can visit and receive blessings from the stupa erected by Kyere
Chökyong Wangpo, as well as his four-activities[2] practice cave,
which is located there.

A prophecy of the Gyarong Tertön Sang-ngag Lingpa states,
"The supreme place of the supreme lamas is found in the direction
of Kathog. Through the Drichu River valley lies the sacred place of
Vajrapani, known as Palyul. The sky resembles an auspicious silken
tent-like umbrella and the earth abounds with auspicious, beautiful
foliage. Vajra-like ravines encircle in all directions, the rock mountains are as black as charcoal, and at the base of the central mountain is a rich forest of trees. The rocks clearly display self-
originating images of *Vajrapani*, as well as blue *Hung* syllables with
radiating flames. Both the unsurpassed practice cave of Yeshe
Tsogyal and the *Sangdag* Secret Accomplishment[3] cave of Padmasambhava are located here. The *Termas Tempo Dondul Drubtab Kor
Sum* (The Three Cycle Accomplishment Practice to Subdue Fierce
Demonic Forces), the Five *Garudas* Accomplishment practice, the
Condensed Life Story of Padmasambhava, and a statue of *Vajrapani*
and Padmasambhava were all buried here. Inexpressible signs of accomplishment and self-originating phenomena are apparent
throughout the area. The unmistaken words of the Vajra prophecy
also state, "At *Nam-tsong* rock (located in front of the Palyul
monastery) thirteen secret *termas* have been concealed." The
mountain upon which the monastery is situated is unusually
shaped, like a proud elephant. It is in this excellent place which, according to geomancy, possesses all the essential signs and where
countless *vidyadharas* have blessed the ground with their sacred
lotus feet, that the founding father, protector of all beings, Kunzang
Sherab, made his spiritual seat.

3 Mahasiddha Karma Chagmed Rinpoche

A Life Story Called Meaningful to Behold

He whose nature is the translator Luyi Gyaltsen,
Delighting in the dance of the illusory primordial wisdom display,
Who postpones the unfortunate calamities
Experienced by sentient beings of the degenerate times,
To the accomplished scholar and meditator
Who bears the name Karma,
I bow down.

The Buddha *Vairocana* encompasses the inconceivable pure realms in the begging bowl he holds with the *mudra* of meditative equipoise. Within the bowl, in the center of the swirling ocean of scented water, twenty-five pure realms of enlightened body, speech, mind, pure qualities and miraculous activities are sequentially arranged. In each one of these pure realms is an entire world system. In the thirteenth pure realm of the mind's mind is our world system of three thousand myriads of universes. Within these universes there are four main continents and one hundred million subcontinents, among which our southern continent of Dzambuling is supreme. It is only in our world of Dzambuling that the one thousand and two Buddhas of this fortunate aeon will come to achieve enlightenment under the great Bodhi tree. On this earth there are twenty-four regions within which the miraculous deeds of the Buddhas will be carried out; among them, to the north, lies the snow land of Tibet. In Tibet's lower province in the Nyomtöd region of Zalmo Gang, close to where the golden river flows gently southward, the great Mahasiddha Karma Chagmed Rinpoche was born.

One of Padmasambhava's prophecies states, "You who are presently known as Luyi Gyaltsen will be born in the heart of Do-Kham (lower Tibet) bearing the name Karma. Adorned by moles on your front and back, symbolizing your spontaneous accomplishment of the three *kayas*, if you, the fortunate one, connect with the profound dharma, the measure of your life will be perfected by fulfilling the needs of sentient beings and increasing the precious doctrine."

As it was prophesied, Chagmed Rinpoche's father was of the ancestral heritage of the great dharma kings of Tibet. His name was Pedma Wangdrag and not only was he an extremely learned scholar, he was also well accomplished in the generation and completion stage practices. Pedma Wangdrag received many visions of Padmasambhava, Dorje Phagmo and other meditational deities, who gave him direct blessings. At the time that he passed beyond this world, Pedma Wangdrag's heart, tongue and eyes remained untouched by the cremation fire. Countless precious relics issued from his teeth and self-originating images of *Mahakala* (with four arms) and the syllables *Ah* and *Hung* were embossed in his bones and teeth.

Chagmed Rinpoche's mother's name was Chökyong Kyid. She displayed all the signs of a primordial wisdom *dakini* and her continuum was wet with love and compassion for all sentient beings. One night, while Chökyong Kyid was carrying this child in her womb, she had a dream that the Protector *Charog Dongchen* (Raven-faced Protector) came to her, clearing all obstacles and blessing her. She also dreamed that she was flying up a valley on a white horse, while she held a butter lamp.

Through the union of their method and wisdom, Chagmed Rinpoche was liberated from the lotus womb of his mother in 1613, the tenth Tibetan *rabjung* year. At the moment he was born, his father, the Mahasiddha Pedma Wangdrag, bestowed Tertön Ratna Lingpa's *Tsegug* (Restoring Life) and *Tsepag Sangdu-kyi Torwang* (*Amitayus'* Condensed Secret *Torma* Empowerment) upon the infant. His father then named him Wangdrag Sung (Powerful Speech) because he had been introduced to the dharma, and especially Ratna Lingpa's revelations, at the moment he entered into the world.

As a child, the young Wangdrag Sung would regularly see gods, spirits and non-human entities. While at play, he would perform various *sadhanas* and create materials used in dharma ceremonies.

At the age of six, his father taught him reading and writing, which he learned without any difficulty and within a very short time, he was reading Milarepa's *One Hundred Thousand Songs*. On one occasion, while singing verses from Milarepa's songs, he sat in full lotus posture and silencing the eight states of cognition, entered into peaceful abiding meditation for an extended period of time. At nine years of age, Wangdrag Sung received many minor empowerments and transmissions from his guru-father, as well as learning daily *sadhanas*, mandala construction, astrology and other subjects. At this time, he became well-known for his keen intelligence in learning.

When he was eleven years old, Wangdrag Sung once again met with his karmic guru of many past lifetimes, the great hidden yogi, Prawashara, from whom Wangdrag received many important empowerments and transmissions. It was during this time that he resolved to become a powerful tantric adept. With this strong determination, from age eleven to nineteen he wandered in the charnel grounds, including *Palri-tseri*, accomplishing the meditational deity, gathering the dharma protectors as his servants and suppressing the four demons and harm-doers. It was after this that Wangdrag Sung began his accomplishment practices with *Kundril Yidshin Norbu* (All Wish-fulfilling Jewels Condensed Together) practice and then *Gur Drag* (Wrathful Guru), *Damchen* (Protector), the outer accomplishment of *De Gon Trelmai Gonpa (Mahakala)*, *Tadrin Naga Lu Dul* (Taming the *Nagas* with *Hayagriva*), *Chagdor, Khyung (Vajrapani-Garuda)* and others. Each one of these root recitation and accomplishment practices of various meditational deities he performed, in accordance with the scripture, for a one month period. During this time, through the intensity of his enthusiastic perseverance, he received true signs of accomplishment for each of the deities he practiced. Maintaining strict retreat, Wangdrag Sung never allowed the warmth to leave his meditational seat and, in order to avoid sleep, he placed his cushion on a small stool where he was forced to sit up during the night, the stool being so small and precarious that if he leaned to one side or the other, he would fall off.

From Kunga Namgyal of Drungpa Tserlung, Wangdrag Sung received the transmissions for the meditation and recitation of *Avalokiteshvara* and *Chagchen Lhenchig Kyejor (Mahamudra)*. After practicing, he told his guru of his realizations and was then given a direct introduction to the nature of the mind.

At the age of nineteen, Wangdrag Sung realized that the doctrine of the unequaled Lord Buddha, the Holy Dharma, which is the indivisibility of teacher and teachings, is dependent on the foundational *vinaya* (code of ethics). Understanding how difficult it is to achieve a precious human rebirth and how easily this opportunity is lost, he resolved to renounce family life in order to spend this precious life practicing pure dharma without any distractions.

On the fourteenth day of the first month of that year, Wangdrag Sung took refuge and *genyen* (lay) vows from Drungpa Kunga Namgyal. He then received the name Karma Samdrub. On the fifteenth day of the tenth month of that same year, he traveled to the seat of the Karmapa at Tsurphu monastery. Within the great temple, containing the incomparable statue of the Lord Buddha that had been built by the miraculous activities of the second Karmapa Karma Pakshi, and in the presence of countless other supports of the Three Jewels of Refuge, Karma Samdrub took *getsul* (novice) ordination. His ordination master was the great *khenpo* and *vinaya* master, Palden Garwang Chökyi Wangchuk Chöglei Namgyal. His *lelob* (action teacher) was Zurri Drungpa Dechog and his *sangton* (secret teacher) was Gelong Nyima. The correct number of monks were present. In the morning he became a novice, receiving the name Karma Lobpon and that very evening, according to the *Solshi Sadhana,* he received *gelong* (full) ordination, receiving the name Karma Chagmed. During the eleventh month of that same year, Karma Chagmed joined the sangha at the Thupten Nyinling monastery of the Zurmang tradition.

Karma Chagmed diligently served the sangha through his body and speech, undergoing many hardships as an ordinary monk. He studied the major intermediate and minor texts on logic, the five principal scriptures of India, Drigung's *Gongchig* (One Mind) and other texts with consistent courage and determination. Karma Chagmed would regularly confer with other great scholars to voice his doubts and clarify his understanding. At Zurmang monastery the *vinaya* was extremely strict and Karma Chagmed never compromised the disciplined quality of his honorable character.

In the year of the Dragon, the Gyalwang Karmapa and his two spiritual sons (Gyalsap Rinpoche and Sharmar Rinpoche) came to Zurmang monastery. During their visit, Karma Chagmed was fortunate to receive directly from the Karmapa the great commentary on *Chagchen Lhenchig Kyejor* (The Co-emergent *Mahamudra*), *Dechog* (*Chakrasamvara*), *Phagmo* (*Vajra Varahi*), *Menlha* (Medicine Buddha), *Drigung Gongchig* (Drigung's One Mind), *Jamcho De Nga* (Five Classes of *Maitreya's* Dharma) and many other empowerments, transmissions and teachings for six successive months. Following this, Chagmed Rinpoche accompanied the Gyalwang Karmapa and his two spiritual sons to the upper region of Tsang to the place called Shelkar Gyang Tser. Remaining there with these precious gurus, he studied very hard for a year and a half. Later, in the year of the Snake, when the Great Prayer Festival of the Karma Kamsang tradition was performed, Karma Chagmed was examined in the presence of a gathering of twelve thousand monks, during which time his fame as a scholar became as all-pervasive as space.

When Karma Chagmed was in his twenty-second year, the Gyalwang Karmapa Chöying Dorje passed into the sphere of truth. Following his passing, some seventy thousand monks of the Kagyu tradition gathered to make an inconceivable amount of offerings in his honor. As it was a tradition for highly realized *bodhisattvas* of the past to offer one thousand butter lamps on their body, Karma Chagmed offered one finger on his right hand as a butter lamp. During the time that he made this offering, Karma Chagmed relaxed the great bliss sphere of the originally pure empty nature of pure awareness. By the power of his dedicational prayer, in the state of three-fold non-conceptual awareness, his merit became equal to the results of *Samantabhadra's* prayers. As a sign of the result of his irreversible accomplishment, several hundred witnesses became intoxicated with overwhelming faith and devotion. Karma Chagmed himself experienced, in a pure vision, the Gyalwang Karmapa bestowing blessings upon him. Seven days later, the physical wound became infected and Karma Chagmed came very close to death. During this experience of intense pain, the depth of his confidence expanded without a single instant of remorse.

While studying Dagpo Rinpoche's text *Thargyen* (Jewel Ornament of Liberation), Karma Chagmed decided to travel to Lhasa, the holy city, to receive the *bodhisattva* vows in the *Gyachen Chödpa* (Great Expansive Offerings) tradition. In the presence of the holy *Jowo Shakyamuni* statue, Karma Chagmed offered a finger on his left hand as a butter lamp offering, following which he received the *bodhisattva* vows. Many astonished pilgrims from Nepal and Mongolia witnessed this devotional act.

Karma Chagmed returned to his native region and built a retreat house at Palri Hill, making this his permanent seat. He daily practiced the *Chöchöd* (General Prayers) and a session of the *Six Yogas of Naropa*. In order to benefit sentient beings, he continually performed special ceremonies for the living, the dying and the dead without any concern for his own personal or material gain. For those fortunate disciples with faith and fervent regard, he offered extensive ripening empowerments and liberating commentaries. Although Karma Chagmed had the power to perform black magic and mantras, he never harmed even the hair of any living being.

It was at this time that Karma Chagmed knew his precious father-guru's passing was imminent and he received from him all the remaining empowerments, transmissions and methods for performing *sadhana* practices. Then his father passed beyond this world and Karma Chagmed used everything he owned to make offerings for his father's after-death offering ceremonies.

He later resolved to accomplish *Thugje Chenpo Gyalwa Gyatso* (*Avalokiteshvara* from the *Nyingma Gyud Bum*) as his meditational deity and twice received extensive empowerments and teachings from Karma Namrol and the mahasiddha-scholar, Lungrig Nyima, both of whom were direct disciples of Gyalsap and Zurmang Garwang Rinpoche's predecessors. One night in a dream, Karma Chagmed received all four empowerments directly from the Karmapa Chöying Dorje, which pleased him very much.

From age eleven until thirty-seven, Karma Chagmed had entered into solitary retreat at least one or two months of each year to accumulate root and accomplishment mantras. Of the Three Roots and dharma protectors there was not a single mantra he had not accomplished. He received many auspicious visions, dreams and signs of accomplishment with *Samantabhadra*, Padmasambhava and various primordial wisdom deities exactly in accordance with the scriptures. Many of these inspiring accounts are clearly documented in full detail in Karma Chagmed Rinpoche's autobiography.

At the age of thirty-seven, in the year of the Bird, Karma Chagmed began a strict thirteen year retreat, persevering in the practice of *Avalokiteshvara, Gyalwa Gyatso* and the *Mahamudra*. Between these sessions he occasionally gave empowerments and commentaries to those fortunate and persistent disciples through a hole in the wall of his retreat house.

At the end of the year of the Horse, Karma Chagmed, through his eye of primordial wisdom, recognized and enthroned the great Tertön Migyur Dorje, whose coming was prophesied repeatedly in the *terma* revelations of Padmasambhava. Karma Chagmed offered the young *Tulku Tertön* (a realized being taking rebirth who is the finder of hidden scriptures) the most profound empowerments and teachings as well as offering many regular prayers for his long life. Through these efforts, many obstacles were pacified and Tulku Migyur Dorje's innate primordial awareness awakened. He recalled countless past lifetimes, had visions of multitudes of deities of the Three Roots and gave oral transmission lineage teachings for which Karma Chagmed was the scribe. Karma Chagmed's kindness to the doctrine of the Nyingmapa was exceedingly vast.

At the age of fifty, during the first month of the year of the Dog, his retreat came to an end. Thereafter, wherever he performed the great accomplishment ceremonies of the *Thugchen Sangdu* (Condensed Secret Essence of *Avalokiteshvara*), *Lama Gongdu* (Condensed Enlightened Mind of the Lama) and others, those present would see *Avalokiteshvara*, smell sweet smells and witness various rainbow-like pitched tents appearing in space.

Karma Chagmed Rinpoche opened the door of the dharma by giving the empowerments for the revelations of *Nam Chö* (Space Treasure) and Ratna Lingpa, composing an extensive commentary to *Sangye Lagchang* (Buddha in the Palm of the Hand), the naked teaching of *Avalokiteshvara Chö Dru Dunpa* (The Seven Dharma Syllables), *tsa-lung* (channels and winds), *Richo* (Mountain Retreat) and many others. Among his foremost disciples were Chöwang Trinley, Pedma Rigzin, Wappa Tulku, Lhopa Tulku, the great Vidyadhara Kunzang Sherab, the Dharma King Ratna Bidza, his sons, and the Nangchen king and his principal aids. More than one hundred disciples achieved realizations and were of great benefit to sentient beings. Gatherings of up to four thousand would attend his teachings and transmissions and the golden lineage of his transmissions continued without interruption.

In particular, the great Vidyadhara Kunzang Sherab received many major transmissions from Chagmed Rinpoche, including all of Tertön Ratna Lingpa's revelations, the extensive commentary to Buddha in the Palm of the Hand, The Seven Dharma Syllables and *tsa-lung*, making these his innermost heart practices. From the time of Kunzang Sherab, all of the great throne holders and greater sangha community of the powerful and glorious Palyul tradition have practiced and upheld this lineage so that the bridge has never been broken; this lineage being the innermost secret jewel treasury of the Palyul tradition.

As the great Tertöns Migyur Dorje and Duddul Dorje had said many times, Karma Chagmed was the incarnation of *Avalokiteshvara*, the Vajra Master Padmasambhava, the Dharma King Songtsan Gampo, Gyalsei Sednaleg, Luyi Gyaltsen and the Mahasiddha Milarepa. More information concerning his past lifetimes has been written by Karma Chagmed in his secret autobiography. Based on this information, one may accurately conclude that according to definitive truth, this great master accomplished the two-fold nature of purity and remains in the permanent state of full-awakening. His ocean-like pure qualities, which ripen and liberate the minds of sentient beings are truly inexpressible. In the eyes of the sentient beings of these very degenerate times, he perfected all possible stages of practice and every single miraculous deed that is possible for the sake of benefiting others.

At the beginning of the year of the Fire Snake, Karma Chagmed was sixty-five years old when, in a pure vision experience, he met the Buddha *Amitabha* indivisibly one as Sharmar Tulku. He spoke to Karma Chagmed saying he was displeased that he had not come. When Karma Chagmed heard the sound of these words, he understood that it meant it was time for him to go to *Dewachen* (The Pure Realm of Great Bliss). Thus, on the second day of that month, Karma Chagmed seemed to suddenly become very ill. In spite of his severe illness, that autumn he gave many final teachings and words of advice to his disciples, once again assisting them to clarify doubts in their practice.

When Karma Chagmed was sixty-six, in the western year of 1678, and the eleventh *rabjung* year of the Earth Horse, he spoke of changing realms. His disciples made persistent requests for him to remain firm and he actually promised to return to this realm on the auspicious days of the waxing and waning moon. On the first day of the sixth month of that same year, with astonishing signs, he condensed his mind into the heart of Buddha *Amitabha*.

For seventeen consecutive days, over one-hundred-fifty monks performed extensive after-death offering ceremonies in honor of the precious guru. The cremation was done in conjunction with the generation of the mandalas of the four classes of *tantra*. During that time, white clouds in the shape of the eight auspicious symbols appeared in the sky and various rainbows, like pitched tents, were witnessed by everyone present. Karma Chagmed's brain, heart and tongue remained untouched by the fire and clear images of *Chemchog (Heruka)*, *Gurdrag* (Wrathful Guru), *Drölod* (Extremely Wrathful Guru) and the syllable *AH* appeared in his organs. In his precious bone relics, the eight auspicious symbols were embossed with images of *Avalokiteshvara Gyalwa Gyatso*, *Dechog (Chakrasamvara)* and *Phagmo (Vajra Varahi)*. These self-originating images and bone relics were used to make a gold and silver statue of Padmasambhava and a one-story high Bodhi Stupa, in order to create the cause and condition through which future disciples could accumulate merit and virtue.

> *Having fully abandoned the delusive net*
> *Of phenomenal existence,*
> *Remaining with ease in the originally pure sphere of truth*
> *The all-good Kuntuzangpo, the Primordial Buddha,*
> *Is the omniscient scholar and Mahasiddha Karma Chagmed Rinpoche,*
> *Possessing one-hundred-thousand marvels.*

* * *

This biography has been written to bring benefit
　to whomever sees it.
Although the words themselves may not be eloquent
　like precious jewels,
The meaning is unquestionably sublime and uplifting
　like the natural quality of the face of a beautiful maiden.
Those who appreciate direct, clear facts
　with the power of the consciousness of mental activity,
Will surely be attracted to this biography,
　without a trace of doubt!

The second Akanishtha Pure Realm,
　the Palyul lineage of Accomplishment,
Is the lineage and tradition
　of the Lord Father Guru and his Sons,
With the strength of a *Chakravartin* Ruler's wheel
　of one thousand spokes.

This tradition is fully victorious in all directions
  over all classes of misguided and perverted beings.
I pray that this place of Full-Awakening
  will remain firm until the end of phenomenal existence!

* * *

This short biography of the great scholar and accomplished meditator Karma Chagmed Rinpoche, was written by Jampal Gyepai Loden (the name was given by Je Khentsey Wangpo), Khenpo Namdrol, with the prayer that the unsurpassed profound truth of the Guru of the Three Times (Padmasambhava) may transfer into the hearts of the human beings of this world. With humility and a pure motivation, this was written at the Palyul monastery in South India, based on Karma Chagmed Rinpoche's own autobiography.

May good fortune and virtue prevail!

4 The Great Vidyadhara Migyur Dorje
A Life Story Called A Seed of Faith

OM SWA TI

In the hundreds of millions of world systems there are boundless illusory manifestations (bodhisattvas) like massing clouds. Among them is Shudpu Palgi Sengi, who is omniscient in the three times and reincarnated as Migyur Dorje, to whom I bow down.

As the condensed self-originated embodiment of the wisdom, power and compassion of all Buddhas of the three times, the Omniscient Orgyen Padmasambhava sends forth countless illusory manifestations into the three thousand myriads of universes, spontaneously arising, without obstruction.

In the realm of *Avalokiteshvara*, the snow land of Tibet, the people produced one hundred thousand excellent accumulations of virtuous merit. In addition, the dharma king, an emanation of *Manjusri*, had an unsurpassed motivation which created the excellent condition for Padmasambhava to come to Tibet and bless the snow mountains, lakes and rocks, creating sacred places for spiritual accomplishment. Padmasambhava fully realized that in the future degenerate times, beings would endure tremendous hardships. With the intention to establish bliss, virtue, glory and endowment, Padmasambhava displayed his enlightened mind as the sphere of the five elements and therein concealed some hundreds of thousands of *termas*, placing them under the protection of the power-possessing dharma protectors.

Padmasambhava predicted the time and place these *termas* would be revealed and who the individual recipients and karmic dharma keepers would be. His manifestations and miraculous activities will be uninterrupted until the coming of the fifth Buddha of this excellent aeon. During this time, Padmasambhava will continue to all-pervasively manifest as great *tertöns* (treasure revealers) who will gloriously work for all sentient beings.

Among the twenty-five principal disciples of Padmasambhava in Tibet, Shudpu Palgyi Senge, who redirected great rivers through his miraculous powers, intentionally reincarnated as the great Vidyadhara Migyur Dorje. In Tertön Ratna Lingpa's revelations, Padmasambhava prophesized, "One with the name Dorje will be reborn in Ngom. Whether or not he makes an auspicious connection with you, Tertön Ratna Lingpa, in the future he will make use of this dharma." In another passage the prophesy continues, "During the time of Chöying Dorje, Tertön Migyur Dorje will come. He will own and control one hundred *termas* in the region of Kham." Another prophecy in Tertön Duddul Dorje's revelations says, "In the future, close to Richen in the region of Kham, one who holds the name Dorje and a treasure index, will be marked by a mole which symbolizes the spontaneous accomplishment of the three *kayas*. Those beings who see or hear him will no longer be reborn in the lower realms."

In accordance with these predictions, which are the undeceiving vajra revelations, Migyur Dorje entered the womb of his mother during the first month of the Wood Bird Year of the eleventh *rabjung* (1645 A.D.). In Tibet's upper province there are three inner regions. The central province has four inner regions and the lower province has six. Migyur Dorje was born in one of the inner regions of the lower province, in an area called Nhom Töd Rola.

His father, Gonpo Tseten, was of the unmistaken ancestral heritage of the enlightened teacher Shakyamuni, Shakya Litsabi and Tibet's dharma kings, who were all descendants of the clear light gods. His mother's name was Sonam Tso and it was through their union of wisdom and method that he was conceived. At the time that he entered his mother's womb, she dreamt of a golden tortoise, radiating light rays in the depths of a vast ocean. While everyone was watching and marveling over this wondrous tortoise, a super-human picked up the tortoise and offered it to her. Gonpo Tseten, Migyur Dorje's father, dreamt that he found a remarkable white conch shell and that he himself was blowing a large copper dharma horn. Unlike the experience of an ordinary pregnancy, Sonam Tso had no physical difficulty and she felt especially blissful and light, like cotton-wool. These were all taken as very auspicious signs.

Just as Lord Buddha Shakyamuni was born without harming his
mother or causing her even the slightest bit of pain, the
Vidyadhara Migyur Dorje was painlessly born on the seventh day
of the ninth month of that same year. His right hand was marked
by an extraordinary blue mole, symbolizing the single-essential
nature of the Dharmakaya. Many scholars agree that the reason he
was born into such a high caste as the ancestral heritage of the dharma kings is due to Padmasambhava's particular blessings and his
predication that "all competent *tertöns* would be born into high
ancestral heritages."

Unlike other children, as a small child he always made dharma
hand gestures such as the lotus-circle *mudra* and threatening *mudra*,
pressing his palms together at his heart and so forth. In addition, to
the astonishment of everyone, he did secret yogic exercises. As
soon as he could speak, he said he was a Kathog lama named
Tsultrim Dorje. He gave detailed descriptions concerning the
layout of the Kathog Monastery, the monastery's customs and the
names of the resident monks, just as he remembered.

One day he had a vision of Guru Loden Chogsed, one of the
eight manifestations of Padmasambhava, and through gesture
transmission, he understood how to read and write. When he was
seven years old, in a state of pure vision, many Primordial Wisdom
Dakinis told him of the importance of relying upon a guru. Instan-
taneously, without any obscuration he had a vision of the great
scholar and siddha, Raga Ah Syei (Chagmed Rinpoche), who was in
solitary retreat, and an intense desire arose to be in his presence.

In the year of the Wood Horse, on the eighth day of the ninth
month, when Migyur Dorje was ten years old, he finally met, with
the assistance of the dharma protectors, the great Chagmed Rinpoche. Chagmed Rinpoche gave him a purification blessing of *Nam
Jom* and *Dor Sem*, and carefully examined all of Migyur Dorje's at-
tributes. He found that he possessed all of the signs and marks of an
unmistakable manifestation of Padmasambhava. Then, Chagmed
Rinpoche gave him the secret teachings on *Thug Drub Yang Nying
Dupa* (Innermost Condensed Essence of the Mind Accomplishment)
in five stages. He was instructed to meditate upon the clear light
Mahamudra in successive meditation sessions. When Chagmed Rinpoche taught him the contemplations upon the precious human rebirth so difficult to obtain, the impermanence of life, cause and
result and the faults of cyclic existence, Migyur Dorje kept

repeating, "I know, I know." He had full comprehension of these teachings prior to receiving them. While receiving teachings on the generation of mercy and compassion for all sentient beings (*bodhicitta*), tears streamed down his face. Many astonishing signs arose to further demonstrate the strength of his innate realization.

In general, in past lifetimes, this Nirmanakaya Buddha had been Kungawa (Ananda) of India, the great translator Berotsana of Tibet, and Shudpu Palgyi Senge, of the twenty-five disciples. His many other reincarnations, according to prophecies, are explained in Migyur Dorje's personal account of his past lifetimes. He actually was already the holder of all empowerments and transmissions that he received. However, like the great *mahasiddhas* of the past, such as Tilopa and others, in order to enrich the confidence of faithful disciples, he displayed himself as a recipient of the empowerments and transmissions.

Initially, he received the following transmissions from his guru, Chagmed Rinpoche: Tertön Ratna Lingpa's *Tsedrub Yang Nying Dupa* (Condensed Essence, Life Accomplishment), *Gur Drag Me Khyil* (Wrathful Guru *Sadhana*), *Thugchen Sangdu* (Secret Essence of *Avalokiteshvara*), Tertön Karma Lingpa's *Shi-Tro* (Peaceful-Wrathful Deities), *Dzogchen Khandro Nyingthig* (Great Perfection-Heart Essence of the *Dakini*), *Ka-gyed Sang Dzog* (Perfected Secret Eight *Herukas*) and *Ta Nag Sog Wang* (Life Empowerment of Black *Hayagriva*). According to the scripture which lists all transmissions received by Migyur Dorje, the amount of ripening empowerments, liberating commentaries and transmissions which he received from the lineages of *kama* and *terma* is exceedingly vast. While receiving these transmissions, Migyur Dorje also memorized prayers, learned Tibetan script, calligraphy, studied the construction of mandalas, and basically trained in all fields of study fundamental to the Nyingmapa tradition. Effortlessly, he developed profound knowledge in all subjects.

In his eleventh year, the year of the Wood Sheep, on the ninth day of the first month, Migyur Dorje entered into retreat with the Mahasiddha Chagmed Rinpoche. While practicing Tertön Ratna Lingpa's *Tsedrub Sangdu* (Condensed Secret Life Accomplishment) and accomplishing the extensive mandala, he received continual visions of Buddha *Amitayus*, Padmasambhava, *Red Hayagriva*, the sixteen *Arhats*, *Amitabha*, *Avalokiteshvara* and many other meditational deities. He received many visions of the protectors

Vishnu, Mahakala, the *Red Damchan Garwa* and others who appeared to be very pleased. The signs of his accomplishment of the practice arose when he stopped an eclipse of the moon by holding his vital air. Unobstructedly, he was able to know what was in the minds of others. He recalled hundreds of thousands of aeons of time and spoke specifically of each of the Buddhas who had come, their names, where they traveled and taught, their parent's names, their activities, their difficulties and their accomplishments. Concerning this, specific details are given in Migyur Dorje's secret life story.

Even in these degenerate, difficult times, sentient beings accumulate hundreds and thousands of virtuous deeds, which come to bear fruit according to the undeceiving law of cause and result. By the fruit of this virtue and merit, Migyur Dorje had a vision of the Primordial *Dharmakaya* Buddha, *Samantabhadra.* Through a sign, he gave Migyur Dorje the empowerment called *Tsewang Dudtsi Gegsel* (Long Life Empowerment of the Nectar Which Clarifies Obstructing Forces). Then the *Sambhogakaya Avalokiteshvara* appeared and, according to the tradition of *Thugje Chenpo Gye-ü,* gave Migyur Dorje extensive empowerments. *Amitabha* gave him the empowerment and transmission of *Drubtab Gyatso* (Ocean of Accomplishment Methods), which includes some forty deities. This entire empowerment and transmission was written down. Then Padmasambhava directly transmitted the four empowerments, followed by a daily bestowal of empowerments, sadhanas and oral instructions of the principal meditational deities who were manifestations of himself. All of these transmissions were written down. In addition, the primordial wisdom and worldly dharma protectors transmitted each of their individual *sadhanas* and authorization empowerments, which were written down individually. All of these writings were collected into thirteen great volumes called *Nam Chö* (Space Treasures). Then Tertön Migyur Dorje practiced, fully accomplished and realized each of these secret treasures. He predicted that the designated dharma keepers of these treasures were the realized Pedma Rigzin, the great Mahasiddha Raga Ah Sye (Karma Chagmed Rinpoche) and Trinley Döndrub. It was to these three dharma keepers that he revealed for the first time the Mandala of *Avalokiteshvara.* During this time he once again received pure visions of the primordial wisdom and worldly protectors, like clouds gathered in space. He witnessed major and minor gods, demons, and local spirits, all covering the earth like particles of dust, laughing so loud it sounded like thunder. When he asked for what reason they were laughing, they replied, "We are overjoyed that the Buddha's Doctrine is being propagated once again." They then promised to protect the Doctrine of the *Nam Chö* and individually offered their root heart mantras. Thus, the auspicious connection was made for the door of this doctrine to open in an extremely vast way.

In Tertön Ratna Lingpa's revelations, Padmasambhava said that there are actual signs which determine a truly qualified *tertön* (treasure revealer). Some of these signs include the gathering of fortunate disciples with previous karmic connections, the gathering of scholars and *siddhas* with pure qualities and the gathering of faithful male and female disciples who are of good birth and who have excellent attitudes.

As it was foretold directly and through the lineage, Tertön Migyur Dorje several times over during his lifetime transmitted a great river of ripening empowerments, liberating commentaries and transmissions of the *Nam Chö*, the *kama* and the *terma*. Those dharma keepers with karma from past prayers, who were assisted by the *dakinis* and dharma protectors include: Je Drungpa Rinpoche, Tulku Gelong Nyingpo, Garwang Konchog Tendzin (the local king), Tashi Karma Tenkyong, Tsonsar Lama Karma Tenkyong, Jangdra Lama Gyatso, Puba Bhaka Tulku, Lama Damchö Palzang, the great Mahasiddha Raga Ah Sye, the realized Pedma Rigzin, Trinley Döndrub, Yangdag Tutob and the great Vidyadhara Kunzang Sherab. With these principal dharma keepers passing on the transmissions, these *termas* were transmitted and practiced primarily by the greater sangha communities of the Gyalwang Karmapa's monastery, Kathog monastery and Palyul monastery. Fortunate disciples with previous karma came from all corners of Tibet to receive these transmissions and embrace them as the secret treasure of their hearts. Through the realization and miraculous activities of these practitioners the *Nam Chö* revelations permeated every direction. The great Vidyadhara Migyur Dorje also gave many of his principal disciples full accounts of their past lifetimes from the treasure of his mind. He told Tulku Rinchen Namgyal that he was a reincarnation of Sogpo Lhapal. He revealed the location of many sacred places for practice and cared for and protected countless beings.

Although Tertön Migyur Dorje was destined to reveal earth *termas*, the merit of sentient beings was deficient and it was due to this that his presence in this world was cut short. In 1667, the year of the Fire Sheep, he was in his twenty-third year and while staying in a sacred place in Mugsang, he began to show signs of illness. As the third month aproached, his illness grew worse and he was forced to stop giving all dharma transmissions. On the eleventh day of that month, he prayed to the meditational deities and offered many dedicational prayers. He then gave his final words of advice to his many disciples who had gathered. On the fourteenth day, he had a vision of all eight *Herukas* and their accomplishment mandalas. On the morning of the fifteenth day, he beheld the three root-peaceful and wrathful assemblies of deities and assuming the *vajra asana* (full lotus posture) he entered into meditative equipoise. On the evening of the sixteenth day, while counting mantras on his prayer beads, he passed into the empty sphere of truth and remained sitting upright in meditative equipoise for three days.

A large congregation of his fortunate disciples made clouds of inconceivable offerings to his holy body for an extended period of time. According to the tradition, all the necessary fire offering substances were gathered and in the presence of many great *siddhas*, scholars and hundreds of laymen, his holy body was cremated. There were many cries of grief and sorrow as this was being done. During the cremation, astonishing signs were witnessed by all. Rainbows appeared like pitched tents in a pristine clear sky. Migyur Dorje's heart and tongue remained intact in the fire, so that future disciples could accumulate merit. His bone relics were marked with the vowels and consonants of the Tibetan language. These precious remains of Tertön Migyur Dorje's body were placed inside numerous one-story high golden stupas which were built and offered by the great lamas of Mugsang, Bumtsong, Palyul and Riwoche. These great stupas became the objects of refuge and circumambulation for humans and spirits in order for them to accumulate merit.

In general, this great Vidyadhara had so many lineage-holding disciples in the snow land of Tibet who fully accomplished the generation and completion stages that it is inexpressible. Because the protector of sentient beings, the great Vidyadhara Kunzang Sherab, was one of Tertön Migyur Dorje's principal dharma keepers and successors, the successive throne holders and greater sangha community of the Palyul tradition maintained the *Nam Chö* revelations as their principal practice. These methods include the preliminary practices performed to purify and accumulate, the root recitations and accomplishment practices, the *yogic* training of channels and winds, and the actual practices of the Great Perfection, *trekchöd* and *togyal*. The Palyul tradition hosts an unbroken line of pure-awareness holders who have fully accomplished these practices. Due to this, the Palyul tradition has come to be known as the tradition of accomplishment. In addition, the Palyul tradition became an object of praise of many of the great scholars of Tibet such as the lord of dharma Paltrul Rinpoche and the great Jamgon Kongtrul Rinpoche.

This Sprout of Faith is watered by many beings
Whose qualities continuously flow
Like rivers from Lake Manasarowara.
May this astonishing life story,
Like the eight qualities of pure water,
Increase all beings' achievement
Of the omniscient, originally pure immutable state!

*   *   *

This account of the great Vidyadhara Migyur Dorje's life activities is merely a seed planted to assist beings in making a connection. This information was based on a much more extensive biography written by Chagmed Rinpoche. These days there are many faithful aspirants in the western world who are extremely interested in practicing dharma. It is for this reason that I, Khenpo Namdrol, wrote this at the present seat of the Palyul tradition, Palyul Namdroling monastery, in South India, for the sake of benefiting all sentient beings.

May virtue prevail!

5 The Great Vidyadhara Kunzang Sherab

The First Throne Holder

In the originally pure, self-liberated great pure-awareness nature of the primordial Buddha, the state of full-awakening is actualized. Even though the head of all Buddha families is indivisible with this primordial nature, countless displays of primordial wisdom are manifested, like limitless clouds, for the sake of taming sentient beings. The protector of all sentient beings, the great Vidyadhara Kunzang Sherab, had many incarnations, manifesting both successively and simultaneously. Some of his past incarnations include Drachen-dzin (the son of the unequalled teacher, Buddha Shakyamuni); the *Arhat* Genyen Dharmata (one of the sixteen *Arhats*, who was an emanation of *Avalokiteshvara*); Garab Dorje (the teacher of *Ati Yoga*); Shiri Singha (the great *Vajra Acharya* of the *Ati Yoga*); Jampal Shenyen (the scholar); King Indrabhuti (the later lineage holder); the accomplished Hashang of China; Lasum Gyalwa Changchub (also known as Neten Gendun Zangpo of the twenty-five disciples); Chö-lo-gon (an emanation of Aryapalo); Zurchen Shakya Jungney (the omniscient one); Lan Shakya Zangpo; Putowa Rinchen Sal; Taglung Thangpa Tashi Pal; Chag Zompa (a great *mahasiddha*); Melong Dorje (a great *mahasiddha*); and Sherab Gyaltsen of Dolpo.

A special secret prophecy in Terton Sangye Lingpa's *Gongdu* revelation states, "Now this *Arhat*, Gendun Zangpo, by the compassion of the king, will hold the secret treasury of *Gongdu* (One Great Expanse of the Enlightened Mind) in his heart. In order to spread forth the *Gongdu* he will, in the future, bear the name *Prajna* (Wisdom). By maintaining the profound meaning of the *Gongdu* dharma, he will care for sentient beings who dwell where there is no dharma and even worse. He will assume the appearance of a hidden *yogi* and, with a clear voice, his compassion will be equal to space. According to the king, the holder of the *Gongdu,* Gendun Zangpo, will incarnate as the second regent of this dharma. When the powerful king expels Lotsawa Berotsana, all the remaining karma will be amassed. Through the intensity and force of Gendun Zangpo's prayers, this karma will be exhausted and (he) will dissolve into the king's heart. In this way Gendun Zangpo will continue to send forth countless manifestations of compassion."[1] This prophecy indicates the name, activities and qualities of Kunzang Sherab. In addition to Kunzang Sherab, many of his later incarnations, such as Gyatrul Rinpoche, Gyalsei Gyurmed Dorje and so forth, clarified and increased the doctrine in various non-Buddhist regions around Gyarong (northeast Tibet).

The prophecy of the dharma keeper of the *Nam Chö* states, "Toward the east or south of here, bearing the names of Chagmed, Tsultrim and Zang, adorned by a mole on the nape of the neck, confer this dharma upon the one with fortunate karma."[2] These three names, Chagmed, Tsultrim and Zang, refer to Chagmed Rinpoche; Tsultrim Gyatso, one of Kunzang Sherab's names; and Mugsang Lama Dorje Kunzang Gyatso.

In Tertön Longsal Nyingpo's revelation *Yeshe Rab-bar* (Blazing Primordial Wisdom) it is prophesied, "Those three with the name Senge (Snow Lion) and three named Sherab (Wisdom) . . ." In deciphering this prophecy, it is understood that the root dharma keeper can be directly recognized by the *tertön.*[3]

Another prophecy of Garong Tertön Pedma Dechen Lingpa's revelation *Longsal Daki Nyingthig* states, "From the western direction of Kathog, an emanation of Chö-lo-gon will manifest as a peaceful *bodhisattva,* to bear the name of Kunzang and elevate the doctrine of the accomplishment lineage." These and other prophecies of the earlier and later *termas* indicate the coming of Kunzang Sherab and the impact of his enlightened activity.

Kunzang Sherab was born in the province of Do-Kham in the region of Bubor. This region is due west of the vajra seat of Kathog, southeast of Mugsang and close to Kangpang monastery, in the area of Palyul. The name of the village in which he was born is Ah-Chög (the supreme syllable *Ah*). As it is said in the *Jampal Tsanjöd* (Praise to the Names of *Manjusri*), "Of all syllables, *Ah* is supreme." According to geomancy, the location of his birth was extremely auspicious. His father's name was Dorje of the Waley family, from the upper region of Droley. Dorje came from a heritage of many precious lamas, including Lama Wangjor, who was the lama of Barkye monastery in the earlier Kathog period.

Kunzang Sherab was born in 1636, the eleventh *rabjung* year[4] of the Fire Rat. As a child, he possessed compassion for all sentient beings and never harmed even the smallest creature. Unlike ordinary children, he awakened his innate primordial awareness at an early age and was gifted with the ability to memorize many prayers of the Kathog tradition.

Chökyong Gyatso, the disciple of Wangdrag Gyatso (an emanation of *Vajrapani*) from Kham-ü monastery, gave Kunzang Sherab *genyen* (lay-Buddhist) ordination.[5] At the time of his ordination, Kunzang Sherab offered the traditional piece of hair and received the name Tsultrim Gyatso. Chökyong Gyatso also gave him teachings on the *Mahamudra*, the *Mitri Tri Drug* (Six Commentaries of Mitrijnana) and many other profound *termas*. At Palbar Rekhe monastery, he met Drungpa Rinpoche, Chönyid Gyatso, and remained with him for five years. During this time, Kunzang Sherab received the *Tsedrub Sangdu* (Condensed Secret Accomplishment of Long Life), *Ngari Ridgzin Yondu* (Ngari Rigdzin's Condensed Essence), *Chagchen Lhanchig Kyejor* (the Profound Teaching on the Co-emergent Union of *Mahamudra*, from the Martsang Kagyud tradition) and many other transmisssions. He underwent great hardships while doing these practices, including tying his head up by his hair at night in order to completely abandon sleep. Sustaining himself on only one load (thirty pounds) of barley a year, he maintained the discipline of *chudlen* (extracting the essence), by eating essence pills composed of *chongshi* (medicinal stone) and other herbs, in place of food. With dedicated enthusiastic perseverance, he was able to actualize realization of the precious oral instruction he received from his teachers.

Kunzang Sherab was later appointed head chanter for the *dharmapala* recitations in Drungpa Rinpoche's protector temple. During the time he was there, he became well known for his skill in ritual and his robust, melodious chanting. Through the force of his renunciation, he abandoned attachment to the appearances of this life. While in the presence of the Dharma Lord Tagla Pedma Mati, Kunzang Sherab received an extraordinary amount of empowerments and teachings on the most profound doctrines and he was then able to sever the bondage of all doubt.

From the vajra-holder Gyawen Konchog Tashi, disciple of both Tagla and Drungpa, Kunzang Sherab received the transmission of the entire *Nyingma Gyud Bum*, including all seventeen *tantras* of the essential class of *Ati Yoga;* the omniscient Longchenpa's commentary to *Sangwai Nyingpo* (Secret Essence) called *Chogchu Munsel* (Clarifying Darkness in the Ten Directions) from Tagla's lineage; the *Dzöd Dun* (Seven Treasures); *Ngalso Kor Sum* (Three Cycles of Relaxation in Pure Awareness); Yungtön Dorje Pal's commentary to *Sangwai Nyingpo* (Secret Essence) called *Salched Melong* (Mirror of Clarification); *Yangti Yidshin Norbu* (Inner Teaching Wish-Fulfilling Jewel); Dungtso Repai's *Yangti Sergyi Dru Chig* (Inner Teaching On One Golden Syllable); *Lama Gongdu* (Condensed Essence of the Lama's Mind); *Kagyed Desheg Dupa* (Eight *Herukas* Essence of the *Sugatas*); and a great amount of additional empowerments, transmissions and teachings.

From Lama Rinchen Dorje of Gyarong Sogmo, Kunzang Sherab received the *Lama Gongdu* (Condensed Essence of the Lama's Mind) and the *Dowang Chenmo* (Great Empowerment of *Anu Yoga*) of the Kham tradition. At this point, Kunzang Sherab became a strong holder of the earlier Kathog tradition. It was due to the kindness of the two lamas, Gyawen Konchog Tashi and Rinchen Dorje, that Kunzang Sherab was able to receive the lineage of empowerments of Tagla, which included teachings and practice instruction which Tagla himself had received in great detail, directly from each individual *tertön*. Because of this, Kunzang Sherab often said that these two lamas had shown him great compassion and his confidence in them was irreversible.

At Bar Khyim Chöjung monastery, from the precious Lama Sherab Gyatso, Kunzang Sherab received the *Drubje Jenang* (Durbje's Transference of Power);[6] *Jenang Gyatsa* (One Hundred Time Transference of Power); Ratna Lingpa's *Thug Drub* (Mind Accomplishment) and other Ratna revelations; a very extensive *Lama Gongdu Drubwang* (Accomplishment Empowerment of the Essence of the Lama's Mind); and the *Dupa Dowang* (*Anu Yoga* Empowerment) once again.

From Dozang Tulku Konchog Gyalpo, of the Drugpa Kagyu school, Kunzang Sherab received transmissions from the *sutra* division of the precious *Kagyur*, the *Prajnaparamita*, the Kadampa lineage, Ratna Lingpa's *Tse Sang* (Secret Essence of Life) and many additional *terma* transmissions.

From many other great spiritual teachers, such as Ma-nyen Yönten Gyatso, Ah Dro Namkha Chodrub, Gyara Namkha Rinchen, and Kunga Gyatso (the *mahasiddha* of Dege), Kunzang Sherab received the entire precious *Kagyur;* the *Lam dre* (Path and Fruition of the *Sakya* tradition); *Shichöd* (of Padampa Sangye); *Jor Drug* (Six Unions) and many empowerments and teachings from both the earlier and later traditions. There are two large volumes documenting all the transmissions Kunzang Sherab received.

After receiving these transmissions, Kunzang Sherab retreated to the isolation of hidden forests to practice and fulfill all of his commitments. Abandoning sleep by placing thorns around the border of his seat, he persevered and endured the hardships of practice until the heat of experience blazed from within. In this way, Kunzang Sherab achieved the signs of true accomplishment on the path.

He later traveled to the isolated Shugag monastery where he developed irreversible faith in Drulshig Tönpa Gyaltsen. Drulshig Tönpa Gyaltsen was a disciple of Mugsang Lama Jadrang, a reincarnation of Drungpa Chönyid Gyatso, an emanation of Saraha. Because Drungpa Chönyid Gyatso had previously prophesied to Tönpa Gyaltsen about his future disciple Kunzang Sherab, Tönpa Gyaltsen accepted him with great joy. Kunzang Sherab then received teachings from Lama Tönpa Gyaltsen on the collected works of many of the earlier Kathog lamas; Tertön Ratna Lingpa's *Guru Dragpo* (Wrathful Guru); Tertön Karma Lingpa's *Shi Tro Kyed-Dzog* (Peaceful-Wrathful Generation-Completion Stage) and many other revelations. In particular, according to the empowerment text *Drangtsi Chugyun* (A Continual Flow of Nectar), Kunzang Sherab received, over an extended period of time, the very important root and branch empowerments of *Dupa Dowang* (Great *Anu Yoga* Empowerment); the *Gyutrul Shi Tro* (Peaceful-Wrathful Illusory Manifestations); and the *Sem De Ah Dön Chö Gyed* (Eighteen Categories of the Mind Class of *Ati Yoga*). During these empowerments, he received the secret name, Thugchog Dragpo Tsal (Supreme Mind, Wrathful Display). Lama Tönpa Gyaltsen gave extensive mind-ripening teachings to Kunzang Sherab on the Great Perfection *Gongpa Zang Thal* (Penetrating Enlightened Mind) of Ah Do Konchog Gyaltsen's lineage. These teachings introduced him to the Dharmakaya nature of mind and Kunzang Sherab spoke of Lama Drulshig Tönpa Gyaltsen as his extraordinary root guru.

Later, while performing these profound practices, Kunzang Sherab maintained the discipline of *chudlen* (extracting the essence), by eating essence pills composed of *chongshi* (medicinal stone) and other herbs, in place of food. He later traveled to Lhasa (the realm of the gods) stopping at Chabdo Ngom Töd on his way. It was there that he came to know of the renowned Vidyadhara Tertön Migyur Dorje and went immediately to receive his blessings. When Kunzang Sherab saw the face of this eminent *tertön*, inconceivable faith and devotion welled up in his heart. Tertön Migyur Dorje gave him all the empowerments and transmissions of Tertön Ratna Lingpa and Duddul Dorje's revelations, and the *Khandro Nyingthig* (Heart Essence of the Dakini). At one point, Tertön Migyur Dorje gave an empty wooden sealed box to Kunzang Sherab and one to another disciple. At night, each placed their box at the crown of their head and offered many prayers. When Kunzang Sherab later opened his box, he found that it contained a four-sided self-originating medicine crystal with radiant five-colored light molecules in the center.

When Kunzang Sherab requested Tertön Migyur Dorje to bestow the *Nam Chö* empowerments and transmissions upon him, he was asked to choose, at random, a scripture from the library. The scripture he chose was the *Avalokiteshvara* volume of the *Nam Chö*. Tertön Migyur Dorje said this indicated that Kunzang Sherab was a dharma keeper of the *Nam Chö* and he then gave him all the empowerments and detailed mind-ripening teachings on *Dzogchen Sangye Lagchang* (The Great Perfection Buddha in the Palm of the Hand). Abandoning sleep entirely, Kunzang Sherab practiced these precious teachings without interruption until he recognized Migyur Dorje to be the actual *Orgyen Vajradhara*.[7] Ascertaining nakedly the continuity of the mind as the originally pure nature of primordial awareness, Kunzang Sherab perfected the primordial wisdom of the four spontaneously accomplished visions of *togyal*.[8]

It was at this point in his life that Kunzang Sherab became an ordained novice monk, under the direction of Chagmed Rinpoche, who then gave him the name Kunzang Sherab. Chagmed Rinpoche also gave him all the empowerments, liberating commentaries and transmissions of Tertön Ratna Lingpa's revelations, authorizing him as a dharma keeper. In addition, Chagmed Rinpoche gave ocean-like ripening empowerments and liberating teachings from both the earlier and later schools. In particular, he bestowed the teaching of his own extensive commentaries on the *Nam Chö Sangye Lagchang* (Buddha in the Palm of the Hand); the *Chödru Dunpai* (Seven Dharma Syllables); *tsa-lung* (channels and winds) and others. While receiving mind nature teachings, Kunzang Sherab systematically comprehended the entire 6,400,000 *tantras* of the Great Perfection. In one instant, he clearly recalled two thousand previous lifetimes and, quickly ascending the highest stages on the path, he had clear signs of realization.

From Sala Sangye Dorje, Kunzang Sherab received the entire transmission of Gangra Lotsawa's lineage of the *Nyingma Gyud Bum*;⁹ the *Do Zamtog* (the Sutra Zamatog); and the *Songtsan Ka Chem* (The Final Instructions of King Songtsen Gampo). After receiving these and many other dharma teachings from various spiritual teachers in this locale, Kunzang Sherab returned to Mugsang.

It was at this time that Lhachen Jampa Phuntsog, through the strength of his karma, merit and power, became the first dharma king of Dege. Prior to his enthronement, the territory of Palyul was ruled by Lithang Tongra Depa, Tsamdo was ruled by Goshi Ponchung and Barong was ruled by Bagthur Khapa. These three rulers surrendered to the new king of Dege and their territories came under King Lhachen Jampa Phuntsog's rule. A few additional territories were overcome forcefully, during which time many monasteries in the lower region of Kham were disrupted and completely destroyed.

In accordance with the predictions of many holy lamas, King Lhachen Jampa Phuntsog and Trichen Sangye Tanpa together built a new monastery and named it Palyul Namgyal Changchub Chöling. Constructed on the site of the ruins of the previous monastery, the land itself had been blessed by the presence of many great *mahasiddhas*. After construction, most of the five hundred monks who congregated at the monastery came from Lama Galtong Tönpa Senge's college of Barkyei monastery and from the Drichu River valley. Lhachen Jampa Phuntsog appointed Serlo Tanpa Gyaltsen to be the head of the new Palyul monastery, but he declined, saying he was an ascetic and much too old to maintain such an important position. Instead, he suggested that Drungpa Chönyid Gyatso's disciple, Kunzang Sherab, be appointed as he had the power to uphold and spread the doctrine in all directions. The king sent a formal invitation to the great Vidyadhara Kunzang Sherab, who was still in Mugsang. Serlo Tanpa Gyaltsen conferred with Kunzang

Sherab and advised him that it was the right time to accept this position. Kunzang Sherab asked his guru, Tertön Migyur Dorje, to predict the outcome of such an undertaking and the Tertön replied, "According to Padmasambhava's prophecy, the time has now ripened for you to work for the welfare of sentient beings. You must go to take charge of this monastery and it will become an exhaustless source of dharma, propagating the Nyingmapa Doctrine." Tertön Migyur Dorje bestowed all the remaining secret oral instructions and gave Kunzang Sherab full authority to uphold the lineage, enthroning him as a great *Vajra Acharya* to ultimately care for the welfare of all sentient beings.

In 1665, the eleventh *rabjung* year of the Wood Snake, Kunzang Sherab was in his thirtieth year when he arrived at the new Palyul monastery to assume his position. Shortly after arrival, he began instituting the foundational discipline of the *Pratimoksha* rules of conduct, the mind training of the *bodhisattvas* (according to the two traditions of Asanga and Nagarjuna), the general outer practices of the *Nyingma Kama* and *Terma* and specifically, the extraordinary practices of the Great Perfection *Ati Yoga*. During this time the three wheels[10] of his miraculous activities swelled like a summer lake.

Once again, Kunzang Sherab journeyed to Nedor to see his precious guru, Chagmed Rinpoche. During this visit, Chagmed Rinpoche gave the vows of full-ordination and Kunzang Sherab became a *gelong*.[11] In addition to his novice name, he received the title Vidyadhara (Pure-Awareness Holder), his full name becoming Vidyadhara Kunzang Sherab. Upon a throne adorned with canopies, victory banners and brocade silk, the Vidyadhara Kunzang Sherab was inaugurated as Chagmed Rinpoche's dharma regent and he was instructed to put on the ceremonial crown and garments of the Gyalwang Karmapa. After his enthronement, Kunzang Sherab received from Chagmed Rinpoche the transmissions of Tertön Pedma Lingpa and Tertön Gud Dhem's revelations; *Karling Shi Tro Kyed Dzog* (the Generation and Completion Stages of Tertön Karma Lingpa's Peaceful-Wrathful *Sadhanas*); Tertön Shangdrom's *Tse Dag* (Owner of Life); *Trowo, Keng-Kong , Charga* (Three Wrathful Deities); Tertön Jatsön Nyingpo's revelations and Minling Terchen's *Thug Thig Tsedrub* (Mind Essence Life Accomplishment Empowerment). He received detailed teachings on the profound practices of Ratna Lingpa's *Thugchen Sangdu* (Condensed Secret Essence of *Avalokiteshvara*); *Thugdrub Kusum Drubpa* (Mind Accomplishment of the Three *Kayas*); *Tsedrub Sangdu* (Condensed Secret Life Accomplishment); *Guru Dragpo* (Wrathful Guru); *Ta Sang Kor* (Condensed Secret *Hayagriva*); and the *Longsal Nyingthig* (The Heart Essence of Longsal). At one point, Chagmed Rinpoche told Kunzang Sherab, "It is prophesied that you are a dharma keeper of Tertön Ratna Lingpa's revelations and through this dharma you will be of great benefit to countless sentient beings." Kunzang Sherab continued to receive all the remaining transmissions for the works of Chagmed Rinpoche, becoming his direct lineage holder. In return, Kunzang Sherab pleased Chagmed Rinpoche greatly by offering him the empowerment and transmission of Longsal's *Guru Dragpo Yeshe Rabbar* (Wrathful Guru's Blazing Primordial Wisdom).

In order to have the good fortune of a personal audience with the eminent Tertön Duddul Dorje, Kunzang Sherab began a journey which was suddenly interrupted when he reached the warring territory of Lhodzong. Prevented from traveling any further, he sent his servant ahead with the many offerings they had carried to present to Tertön Duddul Dorje. Kunzang Sherab began his journey back to Palyul, but attempting to cross the surging Ngu Chu River, his boat sank. Taking his two attendants by the hand, he assumed the *vajra asana* (full lotus posture) and miraculously crossed the river without even getting his body wet. The news of this miracle spread throughout the area and he became known as the 'Kathog lama who flies over water' inspiring great faith in the minds and hearts of common people.

Once again, in the presence of Tertön Migyur Dorje, Kunzang Sherab offered him each and every one of his worldly possessions. When King Lhachen Jampa Phuntsog and his nephew invited Tertön Migyur Dorje to the royal palace, Lhundrub Teng, of Dege, Kunzang Sherab accompanied him. This was the first auspicious meeting of Kunzang Sherab and the king, whose relationship would later be one of guru and benefactor. During this visit, Tertön Migyur Dorje gave many empowerments and teachings to the king.

Shortly thereafter, Tertön Migyur Dorje was invited to Kathog monastery and again Kunzang Sherab accompanied him. During a major empowerment give by Tertön Migyur Dorje, Kunzang Sherab distributed the vase nectar to a gathering of one thousand people. To the amazement of everyone, this one vase supplied sufficient nectar for all who attended without needing a single refill.

Later, Migyur Dorje teased his attendant Kunzang Sherab, saying he had now shown a sign of accomplishment. From Kathog monastery, guru and disciple slowly traveled to Mugsang and the Drichu River valley. In Mugsang, Tertön Migyur Dorje gave the *Nam Chö* empowerments, transmissions and teachings to thousands of disciples. He then gave Kunzang Sherab many precious *terma* substances telling him, "You are the owner of my lineage of secret, profound oral instructions (*Nam Chö*). All of these profound teachings on the Great Perfection and the precious *terma* substances have been given to me by Padmasambhava directly. Now as I give them to you, you must generate a great motivation to benefit the doctrine and all sentient beings." Kunzang Sherab was then formally enthroned as Tertön Migyur Dorje's regent and many prayers for good fortune were offered. Until Tertön Migyur Dorje passed beyond this world, Kunzang Sherab remained at his side as his principal teaching assistant.

When Tertön Migyur Dorje passed away, Kunzang Sherab performed all the appropriate offering ceremonies and erected a stupa to contain the Tertön's precious bone relics. Obtaining the right hand of his guru as an object of refuge, he returned to the Palyul monastery and erected another stupa next to the main temple to contain the relic. In the meantime, the servant that had been sent on ahead to present offerings to Tertön Duddul Dorje returned, bringing with him wondrous sacred *terma* substances and manuscripts of daily recitations that Tertön Duddul Dorje had personally hand written for Kunzang Sherab.

Kunzang Sherab then invited Terchen Longsal Nyingpo to the Palyul monastery to give all the empowerments, transmissions and commentaries of his revelations. During this visit, Terchen Longsal Nyingpo gave Kunzang Sherab a most precious *terma* image of *Avalokiteshvara* in the extremely secret, unsurpassed aspect. He also gave Kunzang Sherab all the original *terma* manuscripts, prophesying that Kunzang Sherab was a dharma keeper of these revelations. In return, Kunzang Sherab offered him one hundred different objects of oblation.[12] With the common understanding that both the Kathog and Palyul monasteries must work together to uphold and elevate the doctrine, Kunzang Sherab and Terchen Longsal Nyingpo held many extraordinary discussions; during this time their minds became one. In the innermost chamber of the Palyul monastery, Kunzang Sherab built an image of Padmasambhava made of dharma medicine and together, Kunzang Sherab and Terchen Longsal Nyingpo consecrated the sacred image. In the presence of Terchen Longsal Nyingpo, Kunzang Sherab vowed that from his present age of thirty-five years until the completion of his life, he would remain primarily in solitary retreat, eating only the mid-day meal at one sitting, never eating meat or drinking alcohol and never coming close to the smell of an intoxicating beverage. Whether Kunzang Sherab was practicing or teaching, he always conducted himself according to the *vinaya* code of ethics. All of his disciples eventually took full ordination (*gelong*) and combined this pure foundation with the profound path of *Vajrayana* practice. As a result, the environment at the monastery and the spirit of the sangha community was exceedingly clean and pure. He imposed a strict rule that liquor not be used in the confines of the monastery except during the *Tsog* offering ceremony. Many of his disciples spent their lives in retreat, partaking of only the mid-day meal and never eating meat or drinking liquor.

When King Lhachen Jampa Phuntsog requested the first Dzogchen Rinpoche, Pedma Rigzin, to come to Dege to correct and reform the Dzogchen practice of view and meditation, Dzogchen Rinpoche visited Palyul and met with Kunzang Sherab. While exchanging dharma teachings with one another, they realized the one-nature of their view and discussed the similarity of the Palyul and Dzogchen doctrines.

Soon after this auspicious meeting, Kunzang Sherab sent Karma Tenzin of Mugsang to the Mindroling monastery to receive the Minling lineage of *kama* empowerments and transmissions. Receiving the transmissions from Minling Terchen and his brother, Karma Tenzin hand copied most of the *kama* and brought it back as an offering to Kunzang Sherab. This original copy is still preserved in the Palyul monastery. This also marked the first time that the Minling lineage of *kama* came to Palyul, creating the auspicious circumstance which allowed the entire *Nyingma Kama* to later be carved in wood block.

Although Kunzang Sherab remained in meditative absorption most of the time, between sessions he gave dharma discourses and oversaw the enforcement of monastic discipline. In whatever way necessary, he skillfully cared for and guided the sentient beings that met him. A great number of his disciples actualized signs of accomplishment through their meditative experience.

By this time, the Palyul monastery was attracting vast numbers of devotees and receiving an abundance of religious objects as offerings. Kunzang Sherab, acting as though he was displeased with these conditions, took two attendants with him to enter into retreat at the isolated place of Lhari Odsal hill. Through pure vision experience he came to known that Lhari Odsal hill was a sacred place blessed by Garab Dorje.

Living in a thatched grass hut, free from contrived activities, he remained in isolated retreat. Gradually, many disciples gathered around him, so that the retreat place also became an active spiritual center.

By this time, Kunzang Sherab's miraculous dharma activities were extensive. He gathered disciples from as far as Mar Kham, Gojo, Sa-ngen, Rangshab, Trom, Chagdud, Golok, Do Ser, Hor Töd, Hor Mad, Shar Gyalmorong, and Gyanag Bragdro. Even the kings of these various regions showed their respect to Kunzang Sherab by making offerings to him and erecting new temples. Each one of Kunzang Sherab's lay-disciples regularly practiced the discipline of the twenty-four hour fast and vow observance,[13] *phowa* (transference of consciousness practice), and the recitation of the six sacred syllables, *Om Mani Pedme Hung*. In all surrounding regions, hunting and trapping of animals was discontinued and meat was no longer offered as food to lamas performing ceremonies for lay people. The rule of abandoning liquor among the sangha was strictly enforced and the practice of virtue permeated every direction.

To enter the path of this dharma tradition, sangha members first take vows of refuge, then practice the foundational discipine of the *Pratimoksha* by taking lay-Buddhist ordination. They then practice the two traditions of mind training to generate the supreme awakened mind *(bodhicitta)*.[14] Through the preliminary practices, earnest assertion is applied to purify negative karma and obscurations and to accumulate virtue and merit. Towards this pursuit, the tradition of the one month preliminary practice retreat and the accumulation of the four-hundred-thousand repetitions is mandatory at the Palyul monastery.[15] Empowerments and transmissions for one's karmic meditational deity, including the generation stage teachings are given and the root recitation accomplishments are performed. The completion stage practices with characteristics is then pursued, which includes the forty-four day *Nam Chö tummo* (mystic heat) practice and retreat. At the completion of this retreat, the aspirant is given the traditional wet cloth examination[16] to see if the *tummo* heat has been generated. This examination must be passed before moving on to higher practices. Then, in accordance with one's mental capacity, the mind nature and peaceful abiding *(shiney)* practice of the completion stage without characteristics is perfected. Following this is the introduction to extra-perception, *lhagtong*[17] of the Nondual Great Seal *Mahamudra*-Great Perfection *Ati Yoga*. The practitioner is then ready to begin the eighty day clear light *togyal* retreat. This is followed by the darkness practice retreat,[18] during which time the practitioner enters into total darkness, assisted by an experienced tutor, who oversees the retreat, clarifying obstacles and increasing advantageous conditions. After these stages of practice are successfully completed and the warmth of the practitioner's meditative accomplishment is undiminishing, the title, *Vajra Acharya* (Master of *Vajrayana*) is bestowed and the *Duddul tong drol* hat (which liberates on sight) is worn. Those practitioners who achieve minor signs of accomplishment and complete all these stages of practice, receive the title *Ladren*[19] and the red hat of the *Gongdu Terma*. During Kunzang Sherab's life, the systematic order of these practices became a tradition at the Palyul monastery and still continues to the present time.

Kunzang Sherab continually gave empowerments, transmissions and teachings to all of his disciples according to the level of their experience and potential. He never taught without first considering the disciples' scope of awareness and the corresponding stage of practice suitable to the individual. From pre-dawn until dusk, he performed his own practices and maintained silence until the conclusion of his final evening sessions. Then he would teach until midnight, clarifying the doubts of both resident and non-resident disciples. Afterwards, he would sleep for the duration of one session, which was three hours. He ate only the mid-day meal at one sitting, and always recited the *Shobul Sutra*[20] as a special food offering prayer. Each morning and evening, Kunzang Sherab meditated upon *tummo* and *togyal*. After completing all the root mantra recitation and accomplishment practices of the Three Roots of the earlier and later *kama* and *terma* lineages, he continued to perform these practices on a rotating basis. Each full moon and thirtieth day of the lunar month, Kunzang Sherab practiced *sojong*[21] and never ignored any of the practices he regularly performed on auspicious days.

Those who came into his presence found him to be exceedingly honorable and without a single shortcoming.

Kunzang Sherab gave all of the personal offerings he received to the greater sangha community to be used to build supports for the doctrine. He supplied food and clothing to disciples who had the potential to meditate, but had no resources to sustain themselves. Saving the lives of all types of animals, he was particularly sensitive toward the suffering imposed upon the *dzo* and *yak*[22] of Tibet, who were, and continue to be, forced to do labor. Kunzang Sherab would give these animals their freedom by offering them to the Primordial Wisdom *Mahakala* and setting them free to roam the mountains.

Kunzang Sherab regularly performed countless great accomplishment ceremonies and dharma medicine accomplishments. According to the ritual instruction of his guru, Chagmed Rinpoche, he began the regular practice of Ratna Lingpa's *Kusum Thugdrub* (Three *Kaya* Mind Accomplishment) and the *Thugchen Sangdu* (Condensed Secret Essence of *Avalokiteshvara*), for which he wrote a new text called *Ngul Kar Melong* (White Silver Mirror). Each year he performed the great vast accomplishment of *Kye Dun Rilbu* (Seven Successive Lifetimes Precious Pill)[23] and wrote a new index for the practice. Kunzang Sherab also began the regular practices of the great accomplishment and dharma medicine accomplishment of *Kagyed* (Eight *Herukas*), based on the *Kha Long Yang Pai Drub Shog* (Accomplishment Format Text) and *Gongdu* (Condensed Essence of the Enlightened Mind), based on the *Cha Khung Drub Khog* (Accomplishment Format Text). The great accomplishment ceremonies of *Kagyed*, *Gongdu*, *Thug Drub* and *Sangdu* were performed each year for four years. All of these practices which are part of the Palyul tradition were established by Kunzang Sherab and have continued uninterrupted to the present day.

Kunzang Sherab was well-known for erecting many *kanika* stupas[24] at the junction of crossroads. He also erected beautiful gateways along the major roadways, painting them with sacred images of deities and with mantras possessing the power to plant the seed of liberation on sight. He produced many special mandalas which, if worn on the body, grant supreme protection and liberation. At the conclusion of the great accomplishment ceremonies over which he presided, the fire offering was performed and the smoke that arose possessed, when viewed, the power to liberate on sight. The blessed offering substances were placed in the great rivers, impregnating the entire waters with blessing powers. In addition, Kunzang Sherab annually performed the ritual of blessing the sun's rays.[25]

Kunzang Sherab gave *genyen* (lay-Buddhist vows), *getsul* (novice vows) and *gelong* (full-ordination vows) to countless aspirants. Innumerable devotees received profound teachings from him and spent their lifetimes accomplishing the practices. When their understanding matured, many were able to recall past and future lives and they possessed the potential to actually bless the minds of others. Many of Kunzang Sherab's fortunate disciples achieved profound knowledge and insight through which their dharma activities were of inconceivable benefit to other sentient beings. Lama Dozang of Mugsang said that he had personally visited nearly one hundred new monasteries and retreat centers which Kunzang Sherab's disciples had built prior to the great *vidyadhara's* passing.

Through the power of prayer, *bodhisattvas* intentionally manifest in ordinary existence. Knowing this, the temporary signs of accomplishment that are displayed for the benefit of reaching sentient beings are in accordance with their various levels of understanding. In accordance with the perception of ordinary beings, the *Bodhisattva* Kunzang Sherab displayed miraculous signs on many auspicious occasions. He possessed the ability to make apparent to his disciples the nature of the discursive thoughts arising in their minds. He predicted future events without a moment's hesitation. Mingling appearances and mind, he left foot impressions upon many rocks, these being visible to the present time.

In the later part of his life, he lost interest in contrived activities and practices, feeling it was no longer necessary for him to build supports for the doctrine. However, with the resources he had, he built a new two-story temple at the Palyul monastery, calling it *Lhasar Khang* (New Temple of the Gods). In recent years, a new iron fence has been built around this temple and the name has been changed to *Chagdra Kang* (Iron Fence Temple). After the completion of the temple, an unusual man, wearing the garb of an Indian *sadhu* (renunciate), suddenly appeared and offered Kunzang Sherab paint for the new temple. With this, Kunzang Sherab painted frescoes of the images of the *Nam Chö* deities at the level of the second floor. In the inner chamber of the temple, he built images of his root gurus and four main disciples, which he covered with gold. He also made a gold and copper image of *Jowo Yidshin Norbu*[26] that was the height of one story. While this sacred image was being built, armies of ants carried tiny balls of gold as offerings to the statue. When Kunzang Sherab consecrated the image, he received a clear vision of *Mahakala* as *Gonpo Ma-ning* encompassing the earth and space and then dissolving into the statue. While performing the dharma medicine accomplishment of *Gongdu* (Condensed Essence of the Enlightened Mind), Kunzang Sherab had a clear vision of *Pedma Vajra*, the principal deity. At the same time, a sprout of the aurura (myrobalan) plant spontaneously appeared in the dharma medicine that was being consecrated. The healing fragrance of the plant permeated the entire temple and monastery. One disciple, approaching from Gaje Tsekhyil Shig (a town about thirty-five kilometers away) could smell the aroma even at such a great distance.

During the consecration ceremony of the three supports of the doctrine, Kunzang Sherab had a vision of Tertön Migyur Dorje appearing in the space in front of him. He then witnessed an inconceivable number of deities, mantric syllables and hand implements radiating from Migyur Dorje's body, dissolving into and consecrating the three supports. While performing the dharma medicine accomplishment of Tertön Ratna Lingpa's *Tug Drub* (Mind Accomplishment), showers of flowers descended from space. All those present witnessed the marvel of three white rings of luminous moonlight encircling the temple and the nectar in the skull cup overflowed with the sound of rapidly boiling water.

While Kunzang Sherab was performing self-initiation, in preparation for giving the *Kagyed Desheg Dupa* (Eight *Herukas* Condensed Essence of the Sugatas) empowerment, several disciples present in the temple witnessed the nine main deities and their asemblies in full illumination, as he performed the deity generation stage. During Tertön Ratna Lingpa's *Thugsang Bumdrub* (Vase Accomplishment of the Secret Essence of *Avalokiteshvara*), the number of sacred pills spontaneously increased, some of which miraculously flew through the air to the river. Beautiful rainbows sprang forth from the temple. Whenever Kunzang Sherab performed any accomplishment ceremony, the excellent fragrance of the dharma medicine would prevail beyond the boundaries of the monastery. Through his boundless activity for the welfare of others, Kunzang Sherab established the doctrines of *sutra* and *tantra*, erected temples and gathered together the sangha community in many areas of China where the name of the dharma had never before been heard. In the past, during the time of Zurchen, Zurchung and Zurchung's son,[27] the monastic seats, lineages and miraculous activities of the Nyingmapa school were widespread. Later, at the time when the Nyingmapa doctrine declined and was in danger of vanishing from this world, it continued to be held by a few mountain hermits and a small number of laymen. Religious leaders of the time, such as the great fifth Dalai Lama, his brother, Minling Terchen, and lamas from the monasteries of Dorje Drag, Kathog, Shechen Dzogchen and others, did what they could to elevate the great secret doctrine, but these efforts alone were not enough. At this crucial point in the history of the Nyingmapa, it was Kunzang Sherab's effortless activities for the sake of the doctrine that caused the spontaneous revival and increase of the doctrine to occur. In the vast region of Kham, Kunzang Sherab was the most powerful propagator of the dharma in general and, more particularly, the tradition of Padmasambhava, the Nyingmapa School. In that context, his efforts were especially important in increasing the three inner yogas of the Nyingma *Kama* and the *Termas* of *Kagyed* and *Gongdu*.

Kunzang Sherab's heart disciples were Pedma Lhundrub Gyatso; Mugsang Dorje Kunzang Gyatso; his nephew and attendant, Tashi Tseten; his younger brother, Pedma Yeshe Gyatso; the four great disciples of Hor, who were Yeshe Senge of Serpa, Ahphel of Janggang, Bag Ding of Shuggang (also known as Raton Lhundrub Gyatso) and Dorje Thar of Tsangda. From these outstanding disciples, the blood and spiritual lineages of this tradition became as precious as garlands of gold, enriching the spiritual heritage and strength of all monastic institutions.

Kunzang Sherab knew that the time for him to leave this world was imminent and he began making various predictions. He especially expressed the wish that some of his disciples abandon worldly activities and retreat to isolated places, such as *Tzari*, a famous power spot, to practice the view and conduct of genuine renunciation. With the exception of this one wish, his expectations for the present and future were fully exhausted. Several disciples did offer to him the vow of renunciation and they retreated to uncertain places to accomplish and actualize the Great Perfection tradition of transferring from this world. It is known that several of these disciples actually accomplished the rainbow light body. Prior to his passing, Kunzang Sherab's final words were directed specifically to his foremost disciple, Pedma Lhundrub Gyatso, to whom he said, "You must uphold the doctrine, just as I have tried to do. You and I will never be apart. Now I am witnessing the descent of a large crystal staircase from space. Like massing clouds, offering goddesses assuming an air of greatness are approaching, leading tigers and snow lions and bearing offering substances."[28] These were his final words. In 1699, on the fifth day of the year of the Earth Rabbit, at the age of sixty-four, after partaking of his midday meal, Kunzang Sherab dissolved the *rupakaya* (form body) into the great sphere of truth.

The moment he passed, the weather became unseasonably warm and sprouts and buds suddenly bloomed.[29] His principal disciples, along with three thousand monks, performed extensive offering prayers in his honor. During this time, the majority of disciples experienced unceasing clear light awareness. While his body was being cremated, celestial clouds mingled with rainbows to fill the pristine sky. A self-originating syllable, *Ah*, became embossed on his skull and many images and precious bone relics were observed. During this special time, many disciples received actual visions of Kunzang Sherab. Others met him in the dream state, some receiving prophecies, the clarification of obstacles, blessings and so forth. A stupa, one story high, made of stone and mud and covered with gold, was erected to contain his precious relics, as well as the *Longsal Terma* of *Avalokiteshvara*.

Kunzang Sherab's collection of personal works include: Buddha in the Palm of the Hand, of the *Nam Chö* Great Perfection tradition of preliminary and foundational practices, with profound teachings on clear light *togyal;* The Lamp of the Doctrine of the Three Vows; How to Rely on the Spiritual Teacher; The Faults of Drinking Liquor; indexes for the great accomplishment ceremonies and many other minor commentaries.

This completes the life story of the first throne holder of the Palyul monastery and tradition, the great Vidyadhara Kunzang Sherab.

In the sky of Complete Excellence
The bright Sun of Wisdom shines over
The land of greater Tibet (Kham).

It is here, in the lotus garden of fortunate disciples,
That the petals of scholarship and accomplishment
Continually bloom and expand!

Kunzang   Sherab
Complete Excellence   Wisdom

Wisdom of Complete Excellence

Tsering Lama Jampal Zangpo.

Mahasiddha Karma Chagmed Rinpoche.

ཨ༠བདེ་རྗེ་འགྱུར་མི་རྗེ་ཨ༠

Tertön Migyur Dorje.

Vidhyadhara Kunzang Sherab, the first throne holder.

ༀ༎ རྒྱལ་བ་དགྱེས་ལ་ཡུལ་འདི་གར་དུ་རབ་གསལ་ཉིས་པ་པདྨ་ལྷུན་འགྲུབ་རྒྱ་མཚོ༎

Pedma Lhundrub Gyatso, the second throne holder.

ༀ༔ །རྒྱལ་བ་དཔལ་སྤྲུལ་བཞིའི་གདན་ས་རབས་གསུམ་པ་རྒྱབ་དབང་པདྨ་ནོར་བུ༔ །

The First Drubwang Pedma Norbu Rinpoche, the third throne holder.

༄༅། །རྒྱལ་དབང་ཡུལ་འདི་གནས་རབས་གཞི་པ་ཀུ་ཆེན་དཔལ་བཟང་པོ།།

The First Karma Kuchen Rinpoche, the fourth throne holder.

ༀ༎ རྒྱལ་བ་དངས་ཡུལ་བའི་གདར་རབས་ལྔ་པ་ཀརྨ་ལྷ་དབང་༎

Karma Lhawang, the fifth throne holder.

ཿ།།ལྟ་བ་དགའ་ལྡན་ལུགས་འདི་གནད་རབས་དྲུག་པ་ཀུ་འཁྱུར་མཁྱེན་དགའ་རྡོ་རྗེ་བསྟན་འཛིན།།

The Second Karma Kuchen Rinpoche, the sixth throne holder.

ༀ༎ རྒྱལ་བ་དཔལ་སྤྲུལ་བཞི་གཉན་དགྲ་རབས་དདན་པ་མཆུ་མ་དོ་སྤྲུགས་པ་བསྐུན་འཛིན།༎

Gyatrul Rinpoche, the seventh throne holder.

༄༅།།རྒྱལ་བ་དབལ་ལ་སྤྲུལ་པའི་གདན་རབས་བཅུ་པ་ཀུན་མཁྱེན་མ་རི་ཕྱག་རྩས་ཀྱི་ཉིད།།

The Third Karma Kuchen, the eighth throne holder.

ༀ༎རྒྱལ་བ་དཔལ་ཡུལ་བའི་གདན་ས་རབས་དགུ་པ་རིག་འཛིན་པདྨ་ཆེ་དངས་ས༎

The Second Drubwang Pedma Norbu Rinpoche, the ninth throne holder.

༄༅།། རྒྱལ་དབང་ཕྱག་ཆེན་ཞི་གནས་ཟས་བ་དཔུར་ཀ་སྐྱེ་ཕྲེག་མ་ཚེ་ག་སྲིད་པོ།།

The Fourth Karma Kuchen Rinpoche, the tenth throne holder.

The Third Drubwang Pedma Norbu Rinpoche, the eleventh throne holder.

6 Pedma Lhundrub Gyatso
The Second Throne Holder

Pedma Lhundrub Gyatso was born in 1600, the eleventh *rabjung* year of the Iron Rat, into the ancestral heritage of Kunzang Sherab, in the Seng-gang area of Palyul. His family name was Gyanag Rawa, which hosted an unbroken line of pure-awareness *mahasiddhas*. A prophecy from Tertön Duddul Lingpa's *Vajrakilaya Terma* states: "As an incarnation of Lhapal, he will bear a mole upon his heart and will be born in Do Kham with the name of *Gya*." As the prophecy indicates, Pedma Lhundrub Gyatso was the reincarnation of Sogpo Lhapal, of the twenty-five disciples of Padmasambhava, who possessed the power to subdue cruel, wild animals by grabbing them by the back of the neck with his bare hands.

As a child, he was known as *Gön Gyal* and at the age of eight, he began his spiritual and scholastic training, which progressed without any difficulty. From the Vidyadhara Migyur Dorje, he received all the *Nam Chö* empowerments, transmissions and concealed secret instructions. At the age of sixteen, Lhundrub Gyatso went to Palyul monastery and remained inseparable from his uncle, the Vidyadhara Kunzang Sherab, who gave him a great number of transmissions and teachings based on personal accomplishment. After receiving these profound instructions, he meditated with intense perseverance and achieved stability in *shiney* (peaceful abiding) meditation. He was then able to remain in the single-pointed, unattached experience of bliss, clarity and no thought.

Taking into account the period of time spent in his mother's womb, as well as the additional lunar months within the Tibetan calendar, Lhundrub Gyatso was able, at the age of nineteen, to take the vows of full ordination, although the mandatory age was twenty years of age. With the correct number of fully ordained monks present, and with Kunzang Sherab as *khenpo* and Tashi Tseten the officiator, he was fully ordained, receiving the name Pedma Lhundrub Gyatso. He was an exceedingly disciplined and honorable monk. In his younger years, he had at least twenty-five tutors, including Palmo Sherab Gyatso, of Bar Khim, from whom he received most of the *Kagyur* transmissions, including the *Prajnaparamita* and the full transmission of the precious *Nyingma Gyud Bum*. In particular, from the great Vidyadhara Kunzang Sherab, Lhundrub Gyatso received the empowerments and commentaries of the *Maha, Anu* and *Ati Yogas*, the *terma* transmissions of Tertön Nyang, Guru Chöwang, Dorje Lingpa, Ratna Lingpa, Pedma Lingpa, Karma Lingpa, Chang Ter, Jatsön, Duddul, Longsal, Migyur Dorje, Longchen Rabjam, Tselei's *Natsog Rangdrol* (Various Methods of Self-Liberation) and Chagmed Rinpoche's Collected Works. After receiving these transmissions and teachings he severed all trace of doubt through the force of contemplation.

When Pedma Lhundrub Gyatso reached his twenty-first year, by the ripening of past karma and with the blessings of the guru, he recognized his true face to be the emptiness-pure awareness nature of the mind, unstained by the confusion of the eight states of cognition.[1] After receiving the mind-ripening *togyal* teachings, he maintained the three unmoving states[2] as the base and accepted the three achievements[3] as the method. Mingling this with the mode of gazing, he practiced the pith instructions. Due to Lhundrub Gyatso's matchless endurance in practice, he perfected the full experience of the four visions. From the age of twenty-five onward, his experience of *samsara, nirvana* and all dual perceptions of phenomenal existence was the nature of the one taste of equality. When he was thirty-five, the founding father, Kunzang Sherab, again taught him the essential inner teachings on clear light without concealing anything. These teachings included the darkness practice, nature of sound practice, dream practice, pure realm training and all the profound essential instructions of the Secret Oral Transmission lineage. After successfully completing these practices, Lhundrub Gyatso received the title great *Vajra Acharya* and was authorized to transmit teachings on the nature of ultimate truth to disciples. Kunzang Sherab announced that Pedma Lhundrub Gyatso, then thirty-eight, was an emanation of a great Indian *arhat* and made him the *khenpo* who bestows the *Pratimoksha* vows. From that time on, he was *khenpo* for the majority of the new monks at the monastery and became well known as *Khenchen* (great *khen-*

po) Lhundrub Gyatso.

As a great scholar, Lhundrub Gyatso possessed non-attached, unobstructed, expansive knowledge about all knowable things. Having actualized the three gatherings⁴ and the three blazings,⁵ he received an abundance of offerings, coming like rain showers. Without any avarice, he used all these offerings to benefit the greater sangha community. Even those with incorrect view developed faith at the very sight of him. He completed the outer, inner and secret root recitation and accomplishments of *Kagyed* (Eight Herukas), *Gongdu* (Condensed Essence of Enlightened Mind), Tertön Ratna Lingpa's *Peaceful-Wrathful Sadhanas*, the root recitations of the majority of the *Nam Chö* deities, the Three-Fold Yidam *Haygriva, Vajrapani, Garuda* and the dharma protectors. He received, in all practices, true signs of accomplishment.

When Pedma Lhundrub Gyatso was thirty-nine years old, the Vidyadhara Kunzang Sherab gave him the following advice: "Whoever is worthy of this definitive truth lineage of Kathog must wholeheartedly uphold it. Without listening to the distracting words of others or ever losing heart, remain here to uphold, protect and increase the lineage of Non-dual Great Seal *Mahamudra*-Great Perfection *Ati Yoga*, the clear light transmissons and the perfection of discipline. By achieving accomplishments in this life, obstacles will never arise and the two purposes will be spontaneously perfected. The time will come when you will certainly see the results of my words." After giving this special advice, Kunzang Sherab gave Lhundrub Gyatso the *Thug Sang* (Secret Essence of *Avalokiteshvara*) and *Nam Chö* protector transmissions, commanding the seven classes of dharma protectors to watch over and constantly befriend him. Following the utterance of these precious final words, the great Vidyadhara Kunzang Sherab dissolved his enlightened mind into the sphere of truth.

After Kunzang Sherab passed away, Pedma Lhundrub Gyatso carried out his wishes by teaching and transmitting the *sutra* and *tantra* divisions of *kama* and *terma*. Based on his personal experience, he taught the generation and completion stage *yogas* and continued all regular traditions of major and minor accomplishment ceremonies at the Palyul monastery. At age fifty-four, he took full charge of the Palyul monastery and increased the number of teachings and transmissions that he gave. Due to his tireless efforts, the doctrine spread in all directions. Without any effort, he received an exhaustless flow of offerings, which he in turn offered to his root gurus, the Vidyadhara Kunzang Sherab, the Gyalwang Karmapa, all of his spiritual teachers and impartially, to the greater sangha community.

In order to make offerings to the representations of the enlightened body, Pedma Lhundrub Gyatso commissioned *thankas* to be painted of Lord Buddha Shakyamuni, Guru Padmasambhava's life stories, frescoes and images of all the deities of *Kagyed, Gongdu* and others. In order to make offerings to the representations of the enlightened speech, he commissioned the writing of many scriptures, such as the entire precious *Kagyur*, the *terma* revelations, *Nyingma Gyud Bum* and the works of many past scholars and *mahasiddhas*. In making offerings to the representations of the enlightened mind, he erected many *kanika* stupas (with the power to liberate upon sight), large and medium size golden stupas (to contain bone relics), 108 silver stupas and many others. All of these offerings to the enlightened state of body, speech and mind were placed within the Dago Lhari Odsal Temple. He then built a large new pagoda with a golden victory banner to adorn the top of the main temple of the Palyul monastery and also an astonishingly intricate mandala model of *Thugchen Sangdu* (Condensed Secret Essence of *Avalokiteshvara*) out of precious dharma medicine for the Lhasar Kang Temple. He made wood block prints of many mantras and images and gathered together hundreds of monks on six great occasions to perform the *Tsombu Tsog Drub Mendrub* (Great Gathering Dharma Medicine Accomplishment). In addition, he presided over the performance of the vase accomplishment on thirteen great occasions. Pedma Lhundrub Gyatso performed countless major and minor accomplishment ceremonies during his life. By his simply expressing a wish to build supports for the doctrine or to benefit sentient beings, it was spontaneously accomplished. Through such diverse methods as blessing the sun's rays, creating images, mantras and supports to plant the seed of liberation through the six ways,[6] his miraculous activities were expansively beneficial on many levels.

From the regions of Gyanag Drago to Chamdo and Riwoche, he was revered by all great spiritual leaders, rulers, gods and men. Pedma Lhundrub Gyatso attracted countless disciples who themselves received experiences such as visions and dreams of the root guru giving empowerments, introductions to the nature of

mind and prophecies. Pedma Lhundrub Gyatso had visions of the
Three Roots and dharma protectors bestowing blessings upon him,
and he could easily understand the thoughts in the minds of others.
He was clairvoyant and perceived in advance all positive and
negative circumstances of the three times, free from obscurity.
Whatever he predicted came to pass. Lhundrub Gyatso could
pacify any illness or demonic force possession by simply focusing
his mind on the problem. Thousands of disciples took full ordination directly from him, abandoning meat and liquor, incessantly
practicing the law of cause and result, abandoning the eight worldly concerns[7] and practicing the three trainings.[8] Hundreds actually
became lamas, with supreme understanding and the ability to be of
direct benefit to others. In different areas around the country, his
disciples built monasteries and retreat centers, greatly increasing
the doctrine of the accomplishment lineage.

When his life's works were complete, Pedma Lhundrub Gyatso
said, "My life is now complete because I have accomplished the
purpose of benefiting both the doctrine and sentient beings. Now
the time has come to train in the practice of the *Dharmakaya* of
death." In 1727, the year of the Fire Sheep, at the age of sixty-eight,
at dawn, on the tenth day of *Sagadawa*,[9] like a golden statue, he
entered into meditative equipoise. In the clear light sphere of the
four states of confidence,[10] he dissolved his *rupakaya* body. At the
time of his passing, in the clear sky to the east, loud sounds
reverberated and flashes of light streaked the sky. During the
cremation, mist turned into rainbows and clouds took on the shape
of images, vases and wish-granting trees. The sound of the fire was
extremely loud and, in the smoke, the forms of deities and their
hand implements could be seen. In his remains, many precious
bone relics were found. Whoever had the great fortune to see,
hear, recall or touch Pedma Lhundrub Gyatso was placed on the
fully ripening path.

Pedma Rigdzin, who was Kunzang Sherab's nephew, also lived at
the same time as Pedma Lhundrub Gyatso. Through his miraculous
power, he traveled to the pure realm of *Khachöd* and was a very
great *mahasiddha*.

This concludes the life story of the second throne holder of the
Palyul monastery and tradition, Pedma Lhundrub Gyatso.

In the originally pure sphere of truth
The spontaneously accomplished ocean-like clouds
Are perfectly placed
To shower upon this garden of the Accomplishment Lineage.
Certainly the lotus flowers of accomplishment will bloom.

Lhundrub   Gyatso
Spontaneously Accomplished   Ocean

Ocean of Spontaneous Accomplishment

7 The First Drubwang Pedma Norbu Rinpoche
The Third Throne Holder

The first Drubwang Pedma Norbu Rinpoche was born in 1679, the eleventh *rabjung*, year of the Earth Sheep, in Chagril, the supremely sacred place near the town of Ahchog. A prophecy in Tertön Ratna Lingpa's revelations says, "To the south of Kathog, a child with the name Norbu will be born." A prophecy in Tertön Jatsön Nyingpo's *Ma-ning* revelation says: "To the south of Kathog, a child with astonishing wisdom and compassion will be born. His name will be Norbu and if he connects with the protector *Gonpo Ma-ning (Mahakala)* revelation, spiritual attainments will be swiftly achieved." The prophecy continues, "The dharma keeper of *Nam Chö Gonpo Ma-ning* will bear the name of *Padma Mani*" (*Mani* is the Sanskrit word for Norbu). These two prophecies predicted the coming of, and assisted in the discovery of, the first Drubwang Pedma Norbu.

Pedma Norbu himself agreed that he was an emanation of the great Pandit Vimalamitra and the Vidyadhara Tertön Jatsön Nyingpo. As a child, he was given the nickname Lhubi. When he was still quite young, he met the Vidyadhara Tertön Migyur Dorje in Mugsang and received at that time permission to practice the *Nam Chö* revelations. At the age of twenty-one, Pedma Norbu met the Vidyadhara Kunzang Sherab and received from him as many teachings as he could. His principle root guru was Pedma Lhundrub Gyatso, from whom he received full ordination and complete transmissions of *Maha, Anu* and *Ati Yogas, Kagyed, Gongdu,* Ratna Lingpa's revelations, *Nam Chö,* Jatsön Nyingpo's revelations and many others.

In short, from his root guru, Pedma Norbu received all the

transmissions of the lineages of *kama* and *terma* as practiced in the Palyul tradition, in the manner of pouring the contents of one large vessel into another. The precious *Nam Chö* transmission, Non-dual Great Seal *Mahamudra*-Great Perfection *Ati Yoga*, Buddha in the Palm of the Hand lineage was given to Pedma Norbu by Pedma Lhundrub Gyatso. Following these transmissions, Pedma Norbu accomplished the preliminary and foundational practices of the stages of clear light *togyal* and he confidently realized the view of original purity, *trekchöd.*[1] He then perfected the primordial wisdom realization of the four visions to achieve the spontaneous accomplishment of *togyal.* Because of these accomplishments in practice, Pedma Norbu received the title, *Drubwang,* meaning Powerful Lord of Accomplishment.

Drubwang Pedma Norbu possessed superior wisdom-knowledge and received a vast number of dharma teachings from many great teachers. With masters such as Kunga Lekpa Jungney of Nesar and Gyalsei Sonam Duetsen of Kathog, he exchanged empowerments and teachings of both the earlier and later schools. He invited the omniscient Chökyi Jungney, Situ Rinpoche, to Dagor (Palyul), at which time Situ Rinpoche performed after-death ceremonies for Lama Kunzang Yeshe, and gave vows of full ordination to two hundred monks.

During this special time, Drubwang Pedma Norbu made boundless offerings to the great Situ Rinpoche. He performed the long life *sadhana* and empowerment of Ratna Lingpa's revelations and the entire *Nam Chö* and *Lama Gongdu* transmissions, in honor of both Situ Rinpoche and his brother, the tenth Sharmapa Rinpoche, Chödrub Gyatso. In return, Situ Rinpoche gave Drubwang Pedma Norbu the *Anu Yoga* empowerments.

At a later time, Drubwang Pedma Norbu built a new retreat center in the lower area of the Palyul monastic complex and spent the majority of his life there in retreat. On special occasions, he would give major empowerments, transmissions and secret essential instructions to extremely large gatherings of disciples. A large number of his disciples achieved true signs of accomplishment in both generation and completion stages, fully perfecting the highest yogas.

Drubwang Pedma Norbu was invited, as royal priest, by the dharma king of Dege, Tenpa Tsering, to visit and bless his palace, known as Lhundrub Teng. During the visit, Drubwang Pedma Norbu said he would perform the *Vajrakilaya* lama dance, from the *Sakya* tradition. Although unfamiliar with this tradition, having never practiced it before, Drubwang Pedma Norbu performed the dance flawlessly and several fortunate observers saw that his feet were not even touching the ground. Simultaneously, Sakya Dagchen Rinpoche, who lived far away in central Tibet, looked toward the east and said, "Today, in the eastern region of Kham, an *Arya bodhisattva* is performing the *Vajrakilaya* lama dance, which will liberate the boundless sentient beings who see or hear of it."

While visiting Dege Changra, Drubwang Pedma Norbu established the tradition of the regular performance of the great accomplishment ceremony of *Thugchen Kyedun Rilbu* (*Avalokiteshvara's* Seven Successive Lifetimes Blessed Pill). His enlightened activities for the sake of beings in these regions were highly praised by many realized beings of the time, such as the omniscient Situ Rinpoche, Shuchen Tsultrim Rinchen and others.

Drubwang Pedma Norbu's principle heart disciples were Karma Tashi and Dorje Tashi of Brag-gang. Many of his disciples achieved full realization in their lifetimes.

Knowing that he had accomplished the great purpose of benefiting the precious doctrine and sentient beings, in 1757, at the age of seventy-nine, the first Drubwang Pedma Norbu Rinpoche dissolved his mind into the great sphere of truth, producing astonishing signs. His sacred body was placed just as it was, inside a large wooden stupa, erected within the innermost chambers of his private quarters, where it has remained.

This concludes the life story of the third throne holder of the Palyul monastery and tradition, the first Drubwang Pedma Norbu Rinpoche.

> *From the astonishing water treasure of powerful accomplishment*
> *Grows the stem of a white lotus flower.*
> *Possessing excellent petals of supreme scholarship,*
> *The fragrance of this jewel is all-pervasive.*

Drubwang	Pedma	Norbu
Powerful Accomplishment	Lotus	Jewel

Lotus Jewel of Powerful Accomplishment

8 The First Karma Kuchen Rinpoche, Karma Tashi
The Fourth Throne Holder

The first Karma Kuchen Rinpoche, Karma Tashi, recalled that he was a manifestation of Tertön Migyur Dorje. In certain prophecies, Karma Tashi is recognized as the incarnation of the condensed essence of Sangdag Dorje Chö; Kungawa; Lotsawa Berotsana; Shudpu Palkyi Senge; the Yogi of Riwo Palbar; Minling Terchen; Gaden Tripa, the Throne Holder of Gaden; Ngawang Chögden, the seventh Dalai Lama's tutor; and the Vidyadhara Migyur Dorje. Specifically, he is said to be the mind emanation of Tertön Duddul Dorje with Gyarong Wontrul Pedma Kundrol Namgyal as the body emanation and Kathog Drimed Shing Kyong as the speech emanation. A prophecy in the Vidyadhara Tertön Jatsön Nyingpo's revelations says, "In the Drichu River valley, a child with the name Karma will be born." In Tertön Duddul Dorje's revelations, it says, "As the speech emanation of Shudpu, in the future I will be born close to Kathog. My name will be Mang-ga (Sanskrit for Tashi) and I shall establish the doctrine of the accomplishment lineage."

In accordance with these prophecies, in 1728, the twelfth *rabjung* year of the Earth Monkey, Karma Tashi was born into the ancestral heritage of Kunzang Sherab, in the town of Ahchog.

From the first Drubwang Pedma Norbu, he received Vows of Refuge and literally, all of the ocean-like empowerments and teachings in the golden dharma lineage of the Palyul tradition.

In particular, as Drubwang Pedma Norbu's closest heart disciple, he received from him the experience-based teachings on the Nondual Great Seal *Mahamudra*-Great Perfection *Ati Yoga, Nam Chö* Buddha in the Palm of the Hand, including secret oral instructions on carrying the clear light awareness as the path. Upon the throne of Kun-zang Sherab, Karma Tashi was enthroned by the Drubwang Pedma Norbu, the thirteenth Karmapa Duddul Dorje and the tenth Shar-mapa Chödrup Gyatso, as the fourth throne holder of the Palyul tradition. He then took vows of full ordination from Situ Chökyi Jungney and received the name Karma Chöpal Zangpo.

Realizing that this doctrine of realization must be upheld through the experience of actual practice, he built new traditional retreat facilities in the monastic complex, below the already existing retreat facilities. These new facilities were complete with private water passageways and doors permanently sealed with plastered mud. With great loving kindness, Karma Tashi cared for his many disciples by erecting innumerable supports for the enlightened state of body, speech and mind and bestowing all major empowerments, transmissions and teachings. Karma Tashi strictly enforced the rules of discipline at the monastery and made many new im-provements. His miraculous ability to uphold, protect and increase the doctrine of the great secret vehicle was phenomenal.

It is prophesied in the *termas* that "China and Gyarong will be at war for thirteen years. In the end, a powerful adept of *tantra* will put an end to the war." During the war between China and the King of Gyarong, Tsenlha Rabten, Karma Tashi was invited to China. King Tsenlha Rabten's guru was a powerful Bonpo lama and by the power of black magic, this Bonpo lama caused a storm of stones to descend upon the Chinese troops. Karma Tashi gazed at the storm of stones and suddenly the storm was reversed. For the sake of protecting the Chinese soldiers, Karma Tashi produced many special protection cords which were so potent that they shook with energy. Not a single soldier was harmed after receiving the cords, which protected both body and mind from the fear of weapons. King Tsenlha Rabten of Gyarong and his Bonpo priest lost the war and, by the force of karmic results, the flag of China flew victorious in all directions.

The Chinese emperor, Chan Lung, was overwhelmed with faith and gratitude and to honor Karma Tashi and inform the people of the Do-med region of Kham of the honor, he offered Karma Tashi an official palanquin and a certificate, written in gold, proclaiming his achievements. The palanquin was exceptionally beautiful, engraved with golden letters written in his honor and adorned with silken banners. The emperor also offered eight precious seals made of gold, silver, ivory, jade and other precious gems to Karma Tashi, which were placed inside a sandalwood and ivory box with eight partitions; each seal having a hand carved snow lion handle. Emperor Chan Lung offered many smaller ivory seals with snow lion handles that were to be worn on the body, and an additional gold lettered document of praise. He authorized Karma Tashi as the royal guru of China and bestowed the title *Tai Shree* upon him. Other offerings that the emperor made to Karma Tashi included the yearly harvest of an entire field of rice, priceless riches such as gold, silver, precious royal treasures and handwoven gold brocade.

When Karma Tashi returned from China, he offered a great amount of the handwoven gold silk brocade and other precious riches to the Kathog monastery. By this time, all the great lamas of Kham were disciples of Karma Tashi, of whom the two foremost disciples were Karma Lhawang and Karma Döndam.

At the age of sixty-three Karma Tashi's enlightened activities were complete and he perfected his mind in the great sphere of truth. The stupa containing his precious bone relics was exquisitely crafted out of Chinese bronze and placed inside the Chag-dra-khang temple of Palyul monastery.

This completes the life story of the fourth throne holder of the Palyul monastery and tradition, the first Karma Kuchen Rinpoche, Karma Tashi, also known as Chöpal Zangpo.

Enhancing the pleasure garden of accomplishment
Is the glorious supreme dharma sun,
Whose brilliance unfolds the excellent petals
In the lotus garden doctrine of transmission and realization.

Chö	Pal	Zangpo
Dharma	Glorious	Excellence

Dharma of Glorious Excellence

9 Karma Lhawang
(the nephew of Kunzang Sherab)
and Karma Döndam
The Fifth Throne Holders

Karma Lhawang was born into the ancestral heritage of the Vidyadhara Kunzang Sherab. As a child, he awakened his pure awareness *Mahayana* nature and displayed signs of accomplishment on the path. Karma Lhawang's childhood nickname was Ahbei Lama and he lived in Kunzang Sherab's personal quarters on the peak of Dzong-nang hill. From his guru, Karma Tashi, he received all the transmissions for the *kama* lineage of the *Maha, Anu* and *Ati Yogas*, the *Kagyed* and *Gongdu Termas* and every essential transmission practiced in the Palyul tradition. Karma Lhawang gave the ripening empowerments and liberating commentaries to large assemblies of disciples and his followers swelled in number like a summer lake.

Karma Lhawang's principal interest lay in uncontrived practice. Because of this, he was relatively unconcerned with the details and responsibilities involved in the running of a monastery, caring for a large entourage of disciples and the general maintenance of the surroundings. Spending most of his time in solitary retreat, he continuously manifested miracles, the sign of his having mingled his mind with the true nature of appearance. In addition, he possessed the omniscience of unblocked perception into the minds of others. When the enlightened activities of his lifetime were complete, Karma Lhawang passed beyond this world.

At this time, the Palyul monastery was in great need of an administrator to oversee the rules of discipline and daily responsibilities carried out in the monastery. The two disciples who took over the monastic administration were Karma Tashi's nephews,

Ah Sam, a realized meditator, and Lama Wangchug.

It was Karma Tashi's direct disciple, Karma Döndam of Pelwar, who took over the spiritual responsibilities of upholding and increasing the lineages of empowerments, transmission and commentaries. Karma Döndam had received all of his transmissions from his guru, Karma Tashi, and he was especially diligent in the practice of the Non-dual Great Seal *Mahamudra*-Great Perfection *Ati Yoga*. He achieved extraordinary realizations through his meditational expertise and became known as a *togden* (realized one).

The life story of this greatly realized lama is rich with the inspiring accounts of his everyday conduct. As a great renunciate, Karma Döndam disassociated himself from ordinary concerns and activities. The fence surrounding his humble dwelling was made of piles of leaves which would scatter in all directions whenever a strong wind arose. His disciples were constantly rebuilding this makeshift fence and they asked him to allow them to build a permanent fence. Togden Karma Döndam always replied that it was unnecessary. In the evenings he never covered the coals in the fire with ash, so that they would still be burning the following morning and he always left the drinking cups turned upside down.[1] As a follower of the great Khadampa masters, Karma Döndam always spoke about the impermanence of life and kept his disciples busy practicing the essence of the path.

When Lhoden Rinpoche, the vajra-holder of Mindroling monastery, came to the Palyul monastery, Karma Döndam learned from him the illusory manifestation, peaceful and wrathful *sadhanas*. Aware of the importance of this practice, Karma Döndam requested that the teachings be given to many other disciples, planting the seed for the foundation of the precious Nyingma *Kama* accomplishment practice in the Palyul tradition.

There were countless occasions that Karma Döndam read the minds of others and accurately predicted future events. In a precious dharma medicine table of contents, some of his hair, taken when he was one-hundred-three years old, is included as a sacred substance. The great Rago Chögtrul Rinpoche said this indicates that he lived much longer than was realized.

This concludes a brief account of the life stories of Karma Lhawang and Karma Döndam, who were both the fifth throne holders of the Palyul monastery and tradition.

This tradition of accomplishment,
Is like the great Lake Manasarowara,
Which the powerful nagas delight in.
Known as Karma Lhawang and Döndam,
Together they adorn the Buddha's Doctrine.

Karma Lhawang   Karma Döndam
Powerful God of Action   Action of Ultimate Truth

10 The Second Karma Kuchen Rinpoche Gyurmed Ngedon Tenzin Palzangpo
The Sixth Throne Holder

In Duddul Lingpa's *Terma* revelation, Heart Essence of the *Nirmanakaya*, it is prophesied, "Whoever establishes a spiritual connection with the manifestation of Shiri Singha will accomplish the ultimate purpose. In the country of Ting or Shöd, where forests and grasslands meet at the foot of a mountain, a child named Karma Gyurmed will be born. Under his right arm, in the front and back, he will be marked with a mole. This dharma should be given to this being of exalted rebirth, who is a tamer of all sentient beings. All beings who see, hear, recall or touch him, after five lifetimes and as one mandala, will be reborn in the pure realm of Actual Joy.

As the prophecy indicates, Karma Gyurmed was born in 1794, the thirteenth *rabjung* year of the Wood Tiger, into the Khanglep family in the Me-chu Gang area of Me Shod. Just after his birth several monks from Palyul monastery were traveling to Lhasa and en route, they stopped to have an audience with the thirteenth Karmapa Duddul Dorje, who inquired about the news from the Palyul monastery. The monks spoke frankly about the difficult times that were being experienced at the Palyul monastery because the reincarnation of the first Karma Kuchen Rinpoche, Karma Tashi, had yet to be discovered. Shortly thereafter, the thirteenth Karmapa Duddul Dorje wrote a letter explaining all the details about the new reincarnation. The letter gave instructions for the new *tulku* to be enthroned at Palpung monastery of Tai Situ Rinpoche, and for the monastic discipline at Palyul monastery to be swiftly restored.

According to the Karmapa's instructions, the second Karma Kuchen Rinpoche, Karma Gyurmed, was discovered, obtained and enthroned. The discovery of the Kuchen Tulku was further authorized by Sakya Drogön Wangdud Nyingpo, Duddul Gyalsei Pedma Wangyal, Situ Pedma Nyinched and other great lamas of the time. In particular, the great Dzigar Dorje Dragpo Trinley Namgyal predicted, "Beyond the golden river and before the town of Terlung, one day's walk through the river's valley, a child will be born in the year of the Wood Tiger, who will have an unusual tiger skin pattern on the skin of his thighs. His father's name will be Döndrub and his mother, Sonam." The young incarnation was found in perfect accordance with this great lama's prediction.

Karma Gyurmed received full ordination from Situ Pedma Nyinched and was an extremely disciplined and honorable monk. From Karma Lhawang, he received all of the transmissions of *kama* and *terma*, as practiced in the Palyul tradition. He received the *Dupa Dowang* empowerment of the Kham tradition, from Serlha Tsewang Pedma Chinpa and was then given the secret name *Rigzin Ngag-gyi Wangpo* (pure awareness holder of powerful speech). From Nyintrul Rinpoche of Kathog monastery, he received empowerments and transmissions for Tertön Duddul Lingpa's revelations. From Jigmed Gyalwai Nyu-gu (the direct disciple of the omniscient Jigmed Lingpa) and Migyur Namkhai Dorje (the fourth Dzogchen Rinpoche) Karma Gyurmed received all empowerments, transmissions and commentaries of the *Longchen Nyingthig* tradition. Practicing the profound tradition of *Longchen Nyingthig* with great faith, he arranged all of the *Nyingthig tormas* of the Three Roots upon his own altar establishing, for the first time, the practice of this tradition in the Palyul monastery.

Like the majority of the great throne holders of this tradition, much of Karma Gyurmed's life was spent in solitary retreat. His principal meditational deity was *Vajrakilaya* (of Duddul Dorje's revelation) and he often had visions of all seventy-five deities in *Vajrakilaya's* assembly. During one pure vision, Padmasambhava came and instructed him to begin the great Dharma Medicine Accomplishment ceremony in the Palyul monastery each year of the Sheep. He also began the tradition of performing Guru Chöwang's pure vision tenth day Black Hat Dance at the Palyul monastery. This sacred dance had previously been practiced and performed only in the great kingdom of Neidong Tsei and at Tai Situ Chöjung's Palpung monastery. To enhance the beauty of this sacred dance, Karma Gyurmed had a great number of beautiful ornate cloaks, masks and essential ceremonial items made from the priceless brocade silk that had been offered to his predecessor, Karma Tashi, by the Chinese emperor.

When Karma Gyurmed actualized realization of the Great Perfection *Ati Yoga,* each one of his disciples simultaneously developed insights by just hearing the sound of his voice. Without any obscurity, not only could he read the minds of others, but he could comprehend their innermost secret thoughts and needs. While traveling to the branch Palyul monasteries of Hor and Gyarong in Do-med, he gave many dharma transmissions and made boundless offerings. In Gyarong, he recognized the incarnation of Kunzang Sherab, Gyatrul Do Ngag Tenzin, as well as Wangchug Tulku, Jigmed Rangdrol (Karma Tashi's nephew). Both *tulkus* were obtained and placed spiritually and materially under his care.

Karma Gyurmed periodically displayed his miraculous powers for the sake of guiding sentient beings. On one such occasion, he focused his mind upon negative forces in order to subdue them and when he threw his vajra, it penetrated through three wall partitions. When he traveled to the hot springs of Tilung, the impression of his footprints remained clearly in the stones, Karma Gyurmed built a new gold and copper roof for the pagoda of Palyul monastery's great Chagdra Temple and he built many new supports for the three objects of refuge. On many wonderful occasions, he transmitted all of the empowerments, transmissions and experience-based commentaries of the *kama* and *terma,* as practiced in the golden lineage of the Palyul tradition. He lovingly cared for all the monks at the mother Palyul monastery, as well as the disciples who gathered from all directions. All offerings that Karma Gyurmed received were used to accumulate merit by supporting the on-going great accomplishment ceremonies.

In 1851, the year of the Iron Pig, on the twelfth day of the fifth month, Karma Gyurmed was fifty-eight years old, when he experienced the presence of the *Sugatas* in every direction of space. Instructing his disciples to arrange many offerings, on the thirteenth day, he dissolved his mind into the great sphere of truth. His holy body shrank to the size of a cubit, eighteen inches in length, while his complexion remained very fresh and life-like. Astonishing signs, such as unusual cloud formations and rainbows appeared in abundance. His principal heart disciple, Gyatrul Rinpoche, built a temple and a two-story gold and copper stupa to contain the holy body of the second Karma Kuchen Rinpoche, Karma Gyurmed. After the body was placed within the stupa, Gyatrul Rinpoche performed extensive offering ceremonies in his guru's honor. This completes the life story of the sixth throne holder of the Palyul monastery and tradition, the second Karma Kuchen Rinpoche, Karma Gyurmed Ngedon Tenzin Palzangpo.

The Dharma of the Vinaya, like the peak of Mt. Mehru,
Is unchangingly adorned by the Sun and Moon of Ultimate Truth
Enriching the lotus garden of doctrine upholders,
This Dharma Lineage is more sublime than the greatest ocean.

Gyurmed   Ngedon   Tenzin
Unchanging   Ultimate Truth   Doctrine Upholder

Doctrine Upholder of Unchanging Ultimate Truth

11 Gyatrul Rinpoche, Pedma Do-ngag Tendzin Ngesang Chökyi Nangwa

The Seventh Throne Holder

A prophecy from Tertön Sangngag Lingpa's revelations states, "The second fortunate rebirth will manifest in the western direction of Kathog. He will be an emanation of the dharma minister Karchen Gyal and will bear the name Maha Tsina (China). With great strength and courage, he will clarify the doctrines of *sutra* and *tantra*."

Just as it was predicted, in 1830, the fourteenth *rabjung* year of the Iron Tiger, Gyatrul Rinpoche was born into the royal heritage of the Chinese emperor's minister, in Tsakho Gyakha Bhoto village of Gyalmo Tsawai-rong.

At the time of his birth, there were many astonishing signs and, as a child, he displayed unusual signs of having awakened his innate pure awareness. While at play with other children, he would hold his vital air and, barefooted, balance himself on the point of a sharp knife. By receiving just one simple gesture, he would comprehend reading, writing and all subjects, as though he never forgot what he had learned in previous lifetimes. Because of these extraordinary signs of accomplishment, it was very easy for Karma Gyurmed to recognize him as the incarnation of Kunzang Sherab and to begin to make the necessary arrangements to obtain him.

When the direct disciple of Karma Gyurmed, Uncle Sangye Yeshe, heard of Karma Gyurmed's arrangements to obtain the young *tulku*, he was alarmed because he knew the custom of that area of Gyarong was to make very generous offerings to the parents of *tulkus* in order to gain their consent to relinquish the child to the monastery. Therefore, Uncle Sangye Yeshe suggested that they only tell the parents that the child was of special rebirth and that he should be sent immediately to the Palyul monastery in order to avoid any obstacles. Karma Gyurmed followed Uncle Sangye Yeshe's suggestion and, in this way, he was able to easily obtain the young reincarnate.

When Gyatrul Rinpoche was ten years old, he received the *Nam Chö* Great Perfection preliminary practices from Lama Sangye Yeshe at Sadu Pedma Odling monastery. While Gyatrul Rinpoche was performing these preliminary practices, he renounced from the very depth of his heart attraction to the pleasures of this world. His conviction to fully accomplish pure dharma was effortlessly born.

At this point in his young life, he clearly recalled his past lifetimes as Rongtön Shung-gya Shakya Gyaltsen and Kunzang Sherab, remembering also the area of Sangphu Neu Thong, where he had previously lived, the exact layout of the Palyul monastery, past events that had occurred there and other additional information. As a child, he often told others that he was Kunzang Sherab's reincarnation. It was clear that the dharma protectors were watching over him and in particular, he was constantly assisted in the accomplishment of miraculous activities by *Ekatsatri*, the principal female protector of the Secret Mantra.

At the age of twelve, accompanied by several monks, Gyatrul Rinpoche arrived at the Palyul monastery. In the Lhari Odsal temple, he was placed on the throne of his predecessor, the great Vidyadhara Kunzang Sherab, and presented with an official letter authorizing the unanimous recognition of his reincarnation. The great lamas who issued this letter were Tai Situ Pedma Nyinched, the thirteenth Karmapa Duddul Dorje and Lingter Pedma Drodul Tsal.

Gyatrul Rinpoche then received the experience-based *Nam Chö* Great Perfection teachings from the second Karma Kuchen Rinpoche Karma Gyurmed, during which time his renunciation deepened to the level of total determination. When he actually received teachings on the naked empty nature of pure awareness, supreme realization arose. After receiving the teachings on the *tsalung* (channels and winds) he discovered the profundity of this extraordinary path.

Other teachings and transmissions which Gyatrul Rinpoche received from his guru, Karma Gyurmed, include the root *tantra*, *Sangwai Nyingpo* (Secret Essence), *Chidon Legshed Roltso* (the General

Meaning-An Ocean of Eloquent Speech) and the *Kyed-rim Zung-jug Nyema* (The Stalk of Non-duality of the Generation Stage). For three years, Gyatrul Rinpoche practiced Ratna Lingpa's three *kaya* mind accomplishment, receiving continual signs of accomplishment. While practicing Ratna Lingpa's great accomplishment of *Avalokiteshvara*, Karma Gyurmed simultaneously gave him all of Ratna Lingpa's empowerments and transmissions. This way of giving transmission is ideal and in accordance with the arrangement of the *termas*. In addition, Gyatrul Rinpoche received all of the *Nam Chö* and other important transmissions of this tradition.[1]

From Jamgon Tai Situ Pedma Nyinched Wangpo, Gyatrul Rinpoche took full ordination and received the name Karma Kunzang Tenzin. Following this, he stayed for two years with the omniscient Jamgon Lodrö Thaye, at the Palpung retreat center. During those two precious years, he studied the Sanskrit grammar book, *Chandrapa*, literature and poetry, and later received the title, Scholar of Literature. He also studied the *Gyud Lama* and many other major scriptures.[2]

At Dzongsar Tashi Lhatsei monastery, Gyatrul Rinpoche and Khentsey Rinpoche together received extensive *Kagyed* empowerments from Jamgon Lodrö Thaye. From Jamgon Lodrö Thaye Rinpoche, he also received all the empowerments, transmissions and commentaries for the great *Rinchen Ter Dzöd* (Precious Terma Treasury). It was during this empowerment that Jamgon Rinpoche dreamed he received a golden chain from Gyatrul Rinpoche, which he placed around Gyatrul Rinpoche's neck. The account of this dream is taken from Jamgon Lodrö Thaye's own life story where he states that the dream indicated Gyatrul Rinpoche would give the *Rinchen Ter Dzöd* empowerments three times during his lifetime. Immediately following the dream, Jamgon Rinpoche bestowed all the protector empowerments upon Gyatrul Rinpoche.

Other transmissions received from the great Jamgon Rinpoche include the *Dam Ngag Rinpoche Dzöd* (Precious Treasury of Essential Instructions),[3] which is the condensed essence of the essential instructions of eight great teachers, the *Dükhor Wangchen* (Great Kalachakra Empowerment) and many other important transmissions.

Gyatrul Rinpoche received from Jamyang Khentse Wangpo the two traditions on the view and practice of *bodhicitta*; all the *Longchen Nyingthig* transmissions; the *Gyud Lug Phurba* (Jigme Lingpa's

Vajrakilaya); the *Yonten Dzöd* (Treasury of Pure Qualities) root and commentary texts; and many other important transmissions.[4] In short , he received transmissions for and thoroughly studied all of the major scriptures of the lineages of *kama* and *terma*.

Through the strength of his contemplation and the blessings bestowed by the meditational deities, Gyatrul Rinpoche clearly understood the meaning of all of these precious dharma scriptures and was able to ascertain the *sutras* and *tantras* by memory, as an exhaustless source of wisdom. He achieved unequalled wisdom knowledge in all fields of study and was especially adept in the major tantric works, such as the *Gyud Sangwai Nyingpo* (Secret Essence of *Tantra*). Advancing his meditative experience in the generation, completion and Great Perfection stages, he manifested the pure qualities and signs of true accomplishment.

Gyatrul Rinpoche completed one hundred million repetitions of *Avalokiteshvara's* root mantra. During the dream yoga practice of intentional manifestation, he traveled to *Avalokiteshvara's* pure realm, Riwo Drudzin, to be in the presence of *Avalokiteshvara*, who lovingly accepted him as a disciple, prophesying the fulfillment of his innermost needs. In other pure visions he traveled to various pure realms, where he met Padmasambhava in the aspect of his own guru, Karma Gyurmed.

In Jamgon Komtrul Rinpoche's prayer to all his root gurus, he wrote, "As a previous throne holder of the Palyul tradition, his service to the Buddha's Doctrine is unsurpassed. Through the accomplishment of *Avalokiteshvara*, the two stages will be perfected and, after seven successive lifetimes, according to the prophecy, liberation will be achieved. To Karma Kunzang Tendzin, I pray." According to this prayer and the prophecy, after seven successive lifetimes, Gyatrul Rinpoche, Karma Kunzang Tendzin, will achieve Buddhahood.

In Gyatrul Rinpoche's life story, there are many accounts of miraculous activities accomplished by the oath-bound dharma protectors who continuously befriended him. As an example, when he would pack articles away for storage, they would have doubled or tripled in number by the time they were unpacked. Gyatrul Rinpoche gave ordination to thousands of monks. He gave the complete Nyingma *Kama* empowerments and transmissions eight times; the full teaching on the *Gyud Sangwai Nyingpo* (Secret Essence of *Tantra*) several times; the *Kagyed* and *Desheg Dupa* empowerments and transmissions six times; the *Lama Gongdu* transmissions three times; the *Kagyed Sang Dzog* (Guru Chöwang's Perfected Secret Eight *Herukas*); all of Ratna Lingpa's revelations fifteen times; the *Nam Chö* revelations twelve times; the *Gongpa Zang Thal* (Penetrating Enlightened Mind) three times; and Longchenpa's *Dzöd Dun* (Seven Treasures) three times. Gyatrul Rinpoche gave the great *Rinchen Ter Dzöd* (Precious Terma Treasury) at Palyul, Darthang and Hor, a total of three times. From the precious *Kagyur*, he gave the transmission for the one hundred thousand and eight thousand *shlokas* of the *Prajnaparamita*. Although Gyatrul Rinpoche was never able to finish the entire transmission of the precious *Kagyur* and the *Dam Ngag Dzöd* (Treasury of Pith Instructions), everything else that he had received he transmitted several times over to countless disciples. In addition, he was known to have transmitted countless undocumented empowerments and teachings at various times. He taught the Great Perfection preliminary and mind-ripening foundational practices on Buddha in the Palm of the Hand a great number of times. Traveling to Golog Serthar, Gyarong and Gojo on many occasions, Gyatrul Rinpoche gave many empowerments, transmissions and teachings in the homes of a multitude of patrons. During these visits, he also made generous offerings to the branch Palyul monasteries located there, giving them new supports for the doctrine and providing them with seed money for important projects. He made many generous offerings to the greater sangha communities and restored old and damaged images and *thankas*.

During Kunzang Sherab's life, there were around three thousand resident monks at the Palyul monastery. During Gyatrul Rinpoche's life, the number of resident monks had dropped to five hundred, with another one thousand congregating on special occasions. This decline was due to the degeneracy of the times, yet Gyatrul Rinpoche always did his best to support each monk by making as many offerings as he possibly could.

The dharma wheel of his enlightened activities included the building of a temple with twenty pillars; a pagoda; a stupa thirty-five hand spans high to contain the remains of the second Karma Kuchen Rinpoche, Karma Gyurmed; two images of *Amitayus*, each two stories high, made of silver, placed one to the right and one to the left of Karma Gyurmed's stupa; one thousand statues of bronze, gold and copper; canopies, victory banners and brocade hangings of the finest silk; silver offering bowls made from one hundred fifty ounces of silver; silver mandala plates, butter lamps and vessels; and a *Vajrasattva* temple erected next to the first temple with an exquisitely crafted pagoda roof. This temple contained an image of *Vajrasattva* that was fifty hand spans in height, seated upon a snow lion throne, with a backdrop that displayed the six traditional ornaments.[5] On the top of the temple he erected a dharma wheel, and deer and victory banners made of solid gold and copper. The central image was surrounded by one thousand Buddhas, each one hand span in height and consecrated with precious bone relics of the Buddha which the *dakinis* had given to Tertön Khyung Drag Dorje.

In the Chagdra Kang Temple, Gyatrul Rinpoche decided to build a three-story gold and copper stupa, which would encompass the original stupa containing Kunzang Sherab's remains. When Khentsey Rinpoche heard of Gyatrul Rinpoche's intention, he said it would be inauspicious to encase the original stupa, and that Gyatrul Rinpoche should build the stupa in a different location. Gyatrul Rinpoche made a large brocade applique *thanka* depicting Buddha Shakyamuni and had the entire *Kagyur* rewritten, as well as four hundred new volumes of *kama, terma* and commentaries. He printed the precious *Tengyur;* had new wood blocks carved for the *Prajnaparamita* (in eight thousand and one thousand verses); printed the *sadhana* practice volume of the Nyingma *Kama* and many other major volumes. Gyatrul Rinpoche had ten and a half million clay images of stupas made, printed thousands of prayer flags and sponsored three hundred monks to perform *bardo* practices (liberation through hearing in the intermediate state) for fifty consecutive days.

From the time of Kunzang Sherab until the time of Gyatrul Rinpoche, the Palyul tradition continued to purely uphold the Nyingma *Kama* lineage of empowerments, transmissions and commentaries. The *kama* tradition of mantra practice accomplishment remained very firm, but the *kama* tradition of study and contrived accomplishment had declined in strength. The third Dzogchen Rinpoche made a special journey to Orgyen Mindroling monastery to learn all of the accomplishment practices and to bring the renewed tradition back to Kham. On his return, he gave the transmissions at the Dzogchen monastery. This was particularly important to the great masters of this time because the original source of the Nyingmapa tradition is the *kama* lineage. Later, Gyatrul Rinpoche in-

vited Khenpo Dorje Rabten (Jamgon Khontrul's nephew) of
Dzogchen monastery to come to the Palyul monastery to pass on
all the newly acquired transmissions. The Khenpo came and taught
all aspects of *sadhana* practice in great depth, including chanting,
musical instrumentation, lama dancing and so forth. Following this,
Gyatrul Rinpoche instituted at the Palyul monastery, the *sadhana*
practices of the thirty great mandalas[6] (all created with colored
powder). Of these mandalas, the following are performed during
the first month of the lunar calendar: the fifth Dalai Lama's *Men
Chög* (Medicine Buddha Accomplishment); *Namjom Tro-Kar*
(Wrathful White *Namjom*); *Tsugtor Drimed* (Stainless *Ushanish*); *Odzer
Drimed* (Stainless Light Rays); *Dug-Kar* (White Umbrella); *Za-Yum*
(Mother Planet); *Dudu Go-ched* (Opening the Door of *Anu Yoga*);
Chagdor (Vajrapani); Cha Sum (Three Sections); *Lha* (Gods); *Mi*
(Humans); *Nyen-Tho* (Hearers); *Rang-gyal* (Solitary Realizers);
Changsem (Bodhisattva); Cha (Kriya); Chöd (Upa); and *Yoga (Yoga).* The
following *sadhanas* are performed during the fourth month called
Sagadawa: Do Tsogchen Dupa (Anu Yoga-Great Condensed Gathering);
Sangye Nyam-Jor (Buddha Union); *Yang-dag Dagam Gupa* (Nine Deity
Half-moon Mandala of *Yangdag); Shinje Shedmar* (Wrathful Red *Man-
jusri); Shinje Khathun Nagpo* (Wrathful Black *Manjusri); Shinje Dong
Drug* (Wrathful Six-faced *Manjusri); Rog's Phurba* (Rog's *Vajrakilaya);
Rong Dzom Phurba* (Rong Dzom's *Vajrakilaya); Gyutrul Shiwa* (Peaceful
Illusory Manifestations); *Gyutrul Trowo* (Wrathful Illusory
Manifestations); *Dong Drug Khorwa Kun Drol* (Liberating All Beings
from the Depths of *Samsara); Pedma Gyadan* (One Hundred Lotus
Flowers); *Lung Lug Tsepagmed* (Sangye Sangwai's *Sambhogakaya
Amitayus);* and *Legden (Mahakala).*

Gyatrul Rinpoche prepared all of the materials used for these
sadhana mandalas from the very best substances, sceptors, *Dhyani*
Buddha crown ornaments, costumes for the wrathful lama dances
and sixteen offering goddesses' dance, hats, cloaks, head ornaments, hand implements, bone ornaments, musical instruments
and others. Even the king of Dege offered the crops from a large
fertile field to help cover the expenses.[7] Although Gyatrul Rinpoche planned to build a scholastic college for the study of *sutra*
and *tantra* at the Palyul monastery, it did not occur during his
lifetime. At Mugsang monastery, he sponsored the regular
teaching of the important *Gyud Sangwai Nyingpo* (Secret Essence of
tantra) and sponsored regular peaceful-wrathful accomplishment

ceremonies.

In 1882, the fifteenth *rabjung* year of the Water Horse, Gyatrul Rinpoche built the new Darthang Do Ngag Shedrub Ling monastery in Golog. Monks from the monasteries of Gyarong Serthar and Hor assembled at the new monastery to study and practice the Palyul tradition and one thousand monks regularly assembled to practice all the traditional accomplishment practices, lama dances, preliminary practices and Great Perfection mountain retreat training.

In the *sutras* it says, "When the doctrine spreads from the north to the north, the auspicious connection will be made." Gyatrul Rinpoche became aware while in a state of pure vision, that the location of Darthang monastery was abundant with precious wish-fulfilling trees, endowed with luscious fruits. The vision indicated that the doctrine of scriptural and meditational realization would flourish at that location and that the lineage holders themselves would be like wish-fulfilling trees, upholding and spreading the doctrine.

When Gyatrul Rinpoche returned to his own Palyul monastery, he built a new temple, leaving Lhatrul Pedma Garwang in charge. He then entered into retreat, while simultaneously continuing to build supports for the Buddha's Doctrine.

When the great Jamyang Khentsey Rinpoche passed from this world, Gyatrul Rinpoche outwardly appeared to be extremely disheartened. He dreamed that a long staircase descended from the sky and that Khentsey Rinpoche was ascending, followed by himself. This dream inspired him to build a large golden stupa and he began to assemble the best goldsmiths. Just as the foundation for the stupa was complete, Gyatrul Rinpoche had a vision of the sixteen *Arhats* and he entered into meditative equipoise. In 1891, at the age of sixty-two, on the twenty-second day of the fifth month, with all the signs of having reached the highest stages on the path to liberation, Gyatrul Rinpoche passed beyond this world. Orgyen Chökyi Nyima and Lhatrul Rinpoche completed the stupa that Gyatrul Rinpoche had begun, to the height of two stories, located to the left of the *Vajrasattva* temple. Gyatrul Rinpoche's entire body was placed within the stupa and all the important offering ceremonies were performed in his honor.

This concludes the life story of the seventh throne holder of the Palyul monastery and tradition, Gyatrul Rinpoche, Pedma Do

Ngag Tenzin.

> *In the celestial garden of Pedma's long tradition,*
> *The wish-fulfilling tree is beautifully adorned*
> *By the branches and leaves of the doctrine of sutra and tantra.*
> *He came to this place (Palyul)*
> *To uphold the tradition of teaching and practice.*

Pedma	Do	Ngag	Tendzin
Lotus	Sutra	Tantra	Doctrine Upholder

Lotus Doctrine Upholder of *Sutra* and *Tantra*

12 The Third Karma Kuchen Rinpoche, Orgyen Do-ngag Chökyi Nyima

The Eighth Throne Holder

Prior to the passing away of the second Karma Kuchen Rinpoche, Karma Gyurmed, he left a letter on his table which said, "My incarnation will be born in Khyi-teng." Aware that his incarnation was imminent, Karma Gyurmed's disciples were confident that the incarnation would be easily located. The new incarnation, Do-ngag Chökyi Nyima, was born in 1854, the fourteenth *rabjung* year of the Wood Tiger. At the time of his birth, marvelous rainbow light rays appeared in the sky and unusual and magnificent sounds reverberated in all directions. Born in the Dege village of Ahlo Khateng, his family name was Dilgo of the heritage of Nyo, who were ministers to the Dege king. The omniscient Chökyi Jungney (Situ Rinpoche) and many other great *bodhisattvas* were also born in the Dilgo family line. At the moment of his birth, Jamyang Khentsey Wangpo had a vision of a vast assembly of *dakas* and *dakinis*, arranging clouds of offerings and predicting that the incarnation of Palyul Karma Gyurmed had been reborn in the Dilgo family home. In addition, they proclaimed that his birth would greatly benefit the doctrine of the three Inner Yogas. The fourteenth Karmapa, the fourth Dzogchen Rinpoche and Gyatrul Rinpoche unanimously agreed that the true incarnation of the third Karma Kuchen Rinpoche of Palyul had been born.

Do-ngag Chökyi Nyima took his Vows of Refuge from the fourteenth Karmapa while he was visiting Palpung monastery, and received the name *Karma Kunzang Dechen Sangngag Chökyi Gyalpo* (The All-Good Great Bliss Dharma King of Secret Mantra). He received the *Avalokiteshvara* Empowerment and Long Life Blessing from Chögyur Dechen Lingpa and was placed on the golden throne of the eighth throne holder of the Palyul monastery and tradition. Taking full ordination from Pedma Do-ngag Tendzin (Gyatrul Rinpoche), it was then that he formally received the name Orgyen Do-ngag Chökyi Nyima. Gyatrul Rinpoche gave Do-ngag Chökyi Nyima all the transmissions practiced in his own Palyul tradition. From Gyatrul Rinpoche he received the profound teachings on the Non-dual Great Seal *Mahamudra*-Great Perfection *Ati Yoga*; the *Nam Chö* Great Perfection Buddha in the Palm of the Hand, including clear light *togyal*; the *Kagyed* (Eight *Herukas*); *Gongdu* Condensed Enlightened Mind); *Nyingthig Ya Shi* (Four Volumes of *Nyingthig*); the entire *Nam Chö* (Space Treasures); Tertön Ratna Lingpa's revelations; *Chang Ter*; Tertön Jatsön Nyingpo's revelations; Tertön Duddul Lingpa's revelations; the *Kama Dupa Dowang* (*Anu Yoga* empowerment of both the central Tibetan and Kham traditions; all Nyingma *Tantras*; Geshe Putowa's Works (of the great Kadampa tradition) and limitless other empowerments and transmissions, each at least four to five times.

Do-ngag Chökyi Nyima received the *Dom Sum Nam Nga* (Certainty of the Three Vows); *Bodhicharya Avatara* (*Bodhisattva's* Way of Life); *Abidharma Kosha* (*Sutra Alankara*) and many other major scriptural transmissions from Washul Lama Sonam Namgyal.

Teachings on astrology were received by Khang-nang Lama Tashi Puntsog and commentary teachings on the root *Tantra Sangwai Nyingpo*, called *Sangdag Gong-gyen* (Ornament of the Enlightened Mind of *Vajrapani*) and *Chidon Shalung* (Oral Instructions on the General Meaning) were received in detail by Dzogchen Dorje Rabten.

Do-ngag Chökyi Nyima received the two traditions of *Bodhisattva* Vows and training; Jigme Lingpa's nine volumes; *Lama Gongdu Wangchen* (Condensed Enlightened Mind Great Empowerment); *Semde Nyanglug* (Nyang's tradition of the Mind Class); the *Dorje Zampa* (Vajra Bridge); Minling Terchen's revelations; and Chögyur Lingpa's revelations from Jamyang Khentsey Wangpo.

While at the Desheg Dupa monastery in Dzong Shod, he received the entire *Rinchen Ter Dzöd* (Precious *Terma* Treasury), the *Gongpa Zang Thal* revelation (Penetrating Enlightened Mind) and the *Gongdu* (Condensed Enlightened Mind Empowerment) from the omniscient Jamgon Kongtrul Rinpoche. From Lhatrul Pedma Garwang, he received the six volumes of Tertön Jatsön Nyingpo's revelations. From Drubwang Drodul Pawo Dorje, he received the *Lama Yang Tig*

(Essential Essence of the Lama), *Gongpa Zang Thal* (Penetrating Enlightened Mind) and all the *Nyingthig* teachings. Drubwang Drodul Pawo Dorje praised Chökyi Nyima, saying that he had realized the full potential of pure awareness (the third vision of *togyal*) and he bestowed upon him the name *Longchen Odsal Namkha Dorje* (Great Expanse Clear Light Vajra of Space).

From Palpung Lama Khawang Tashi Chöphel, Chökyi Nyima received the transmission of the precious *Kagyur* and the *Dam Ngag Dzöd* (Treaury of Essential Instruction). From Dzatrul Kunzang Namgyal, he received Mugsang Khenpo Sherab Palzang's Lineage of *Nyingthig Ya Shi* (Four Volumes of *Nyingthig*) and *Longchen Dzöd Dun* (Seven Treasures of Longchenpa).

From Kathog Khenpo Gyaltsen Odzer, he received Tertön Dorje Lingpa's *Tawa Long Yang* (View of the Vast Expanse) and *Drubjey Jenang* (Drubjey's Transference of Power). The major and minor empowerments of Tertön Rinchen Lingpa's *Terma Thugdrub Lamed Dön Dzog Dupai* (Unsurpassed Mind Accomplishment of the Condensed Complete Meaning) were received from the *Tertön* himself. In return, Chökyi Nyima gave Tertön Rinchen Lingpa the *Nam Chö* transmissions and teachings. Jamgon Kongtrul Rinpoche told Chökyi Nyima that Tertön Rinchen Lingpa was a karmic holder of the Palyul lineage and instructed him to care for him accordingly. From Pedma Gyaltsen (the nephew of Kathog monastery's head lama) Chökyi Nyima received the *Nyingma Gyud Bum* and, in return, Chökyi Nyima gave Pedma Gyaltsen the great *Anu Yoga* empowerment *Drang Tsi Chu Gyun* (A Continual Flow of Nectar), restoring the doctrine of the earlier Kathog tradition.

The third Karma Kuchen Rinpoche, Do-ngag Chökyi Nyima, had received vast amounts of transmissions and teaching from both the earlier and later tantric traditions of *kama* and *terma*. Through the strength and profound quality of his contemplative powers, he realized the fundamental meaning of them all. In order to benefit others, Do-ngag Chökyi Nyima began giving experience-based teachings to the *tulkus* (reincarnated beings) at the Palyul monastery and to disciples who came from distant areas, such as Hor and Go-jo. He regularly transmitted teachings on the Great Perfection tradition of preliminary practices, *tsa-lung* (channels and winds) and the stages of the Great Perfection itself. He bestowed the vows of full ordination on 675 monks, gave the great *Rinchen Ter Dzöd* (Precious Terma Treasury) empowerments twice; the *Nam Chö* em-

powerments thirteen times; the *Gongdu* (Condensed Enlightened
Mind) four times; the *Kagyed* (Eight *Herukas*); *Desheg Dupa* (Condensed Essence of the *Sugatas*); *Kagyed Sang Dzog* (Eight *Herukas*
Secret Perfection); *Desheg Dupa* (Condensed Essence of the *Sugatas*);
Kagyed Sang Dzog (Eight *Herukas* Secret Perfection); Jatsön Nyingpo's
revelation four times; and the entire *kama* several times over. Dongag Chökyi Nyima gave each transmission he himself had received at least once, however the majority were given many times
over.

As a youth, this precious teacher's mind was like pure gold with
his every thought directed towards the betterment of mankind. He
even treated those who possessed few good or honorable qualities
with kindness and respect, as though they were equals. He clearly
perceived the equal nature of all that lives and spent his life in the
service of others. As a man free from divisive, sectarian views, he
would not blame, criticize or speak unkindly of others. Although
Do-ngag Chökyi Nyima yearned to spend his life in solitary retreat
removed from the entanglements of worldly affairs, his precious
guru, Gyatrul Rinpoche, had told him of his personal responsibility
to take charge of the Palyul monastery, and so he carried out his
guru's wishes with unquestioning faith. His entire life was spent in
exact accordance with the advice of his root spiritual guide.

While at the monastery, Do-ngag Chökyi Nyima spent the majority of his time presiding over the many regular accomplishment
ceremonies, as well as bestowing transmissions. He was never
known to rest or take any personal time out, except for the practice
of root and accomplishment mantras which he did while in retreat.
His character was naturally disciplined and even-tempered. He
always tried to conceal his own good qualities, while emphasizing
the qualities of others. It was his lifetime pattern to arise by three in
the morning in order to recite all of his daily practices from both
the earlier and later traditions of *kama* and *terma*. Just after dawn,
he would offer *sang* and *tormas*[1] to the hungry spirits. Intermittently he would perform at least one-hundred prostrations and circumambulations. Although he maintained such a demanding
schedule for the purpose of the doctrine, he never cut his own daily
practice short for any reason. While his root guru, Gyatrul Rinpoche, was still alive, he offered to him every possession he had.

Towards the latter part of his life, the wheel of his dharma works
included building the Thubwang Neten Khang (Temple of the Bud-

dha and *Arhats*) which had an exquisitely crafted golden pagoda; a central image of Buddha Shakyamuni, which was thirty hand spans high, flanked by human size figures of his principle disciples; statues of the sixteen *Arhats;* the four protector kings of this world and Hashang (Hoti of China), each one arrow's length in height; several hundred golden statues; a gold and copper stupa thirty hands high and adorned with precious stones and ornaments; and boundless offerings to the three supports. Chökyi Nyima commissioned a famous *thanka* painter from Chamdo to paint thirty-two *thankas* of the Buddha's life story; eight *thankas* of Terton Migyur Dorje's past lives; and *thankas* of the nine root deities of *Gongdu* and many others.

In Palyul (Ahchog) Rigön monastery, Do-ngag Chökyi Nyima built many statues of gold, copper and precious dharma medicine for the bedroom of Kunzang Sherab. At one time, Jamgon Mipham Rinpoche gave Chökyi Nyima a *thanka* of Rogzom Pedma Khandro, which became his secret practice *thanka.* Mipham Rinpoche instructed him to build a statue of *Rigchedma* (Kurukuli) and place this secret *thanka* within the statue so that it would bring great benefit to the Buddha's Doctrine.

Do-ngag Chökyi Nyima later built a new temple to contain the newly copied, sixty volumes of the *Rinchen Ter Dzöd* (Precious Terma Treasury) and he named the temple the *Terdzöd Kang* (Terma Treasury Temple). He had many other rare *termas* and scriptures from the *Kabum* copied, amounting to one hundred new volumes. After reprinting the entire *Kagyur* and *Tengyur,* he printed over one thousand new volumes of scriptures. Do-ngag Chökyi Nyima also completed all the wood block carvings of the *kama* that had been begun by his guru, Gyatrul Rinpoche, and he made many new blocks of the important regular great accomplishment *sadhanas.* He replaced all the old lama dance costumes with new ones made of fine brocade silk, and he gave the older garments to Ragchab and Gojo-Nyulra monasteries. He made all new offering materials, such as banners, umbrellas, canopies and a huge new tent for the dances. He also made hundreds of thousands of clay stupas *(tsa-tsa), mani* stones[2] and prayer flags.

In the Palyul monastery, Do-ngag Chökyi Nyima began the annual tradition of *yarney* practice.[3] During the first month of the lunar year, he began the outer tantric practice of *Anu Yoga Dupa Do* and during *Sagadawa* (the fourth month), the annual *Anu Yoga Dupa*

Do inner tantric practice in both the upper division of Dago and at the main monastery. On the tenth day of the fifth month, he began the great accomplishment practices of *Kagyed, Gongdu, Thug Drub* and *Sangdu*. He celebrated the anniversaries of the enlightenment of great lamas, the solstice offerings, the *gutor* ceremony at the conclusion of the old year, special ceremonies, additional unscheduled great accomplishments and the forty-nine day *bardo* ceremony. He restored the broken tradition of supporting the twenty-five practitioners in the upper and lower retreat centers. He always used the offerings that he received immediately for the benefit of others.

Constantly persevering in the practice of the awareness of the completion stage without characteristics, he spontaneously accomplished awareness of the originally pure innate nature. The amount of root recitation and accomplishment practices that Do-ngag Chökyi Nyima completed of the Three Roots and dharma protectors of *kama* and *terma* was inconceivable. He said himself that for each one of these practices, he received a sign of accomplishment that was either actual, visionary or in the dream state. While he performed the great accomplishment ceremonies, nectar in the skullcups spontaneously overflowed and dharma medicine pills would increase, to roll down the mandala cord in his direction.[4] During the descent of the blessings section of the practice, actual signs of spiritual attainment were regularly witnessed. During the *Gonpo Ma-ning (Mahakala)* section of engaging in wrathful, miraculous activity, the flesh and blood of the enemy of the doctrine would suddenly appear on Do-ngag Chökyi Nyima's table.[5] He often left his footprints upon stone as a sign of having mingled mind with appearances. He possessed unobstructed power to see through and beyond rocks, houses and mountains and he could hear conversations being carried on from afar. Each one of the *tulkus* that Do-ngag Chökyi Nyima personally recognized became exceptional upholders of the doctrine. Although he received many other extraordinary visions and prophecies, because of his prudent character, these experiences were kept concealed. He had a fervent wish to build a scholastic college at the Palyul monastery, which created the auspicious circumstance for the future occurrence.

Chökyi Nyima's principal disciples were the second Drubwang Pedma Rinpoche, Rigzin Palchen Dupa; Tsetrul Jigmed Chökyi Lodrö; Gyangtrul Pedma Thegchog Tenzin; and Ragtrul Rinpoche,

Thubten Shedrub Gyatso. Many of his disciples became great
scholars and accomplished meditators.

In 1906, the fifteenth *rabjung* year of the Fire Horse, when he
was fifty-three years old, Chökyi Nyima dissolved into the exhaustless sphere of clear light. The omniscient Kathogpa Situ Rinpoche, Chökyi Gyatso, was invited to Palyul and together with the
tulkus and lamas of the Palyul monastery, he performed the cremation offering ceremony. During the ceremony, clouds in the shape
of pitched tents appeared in the luminously clear sky, releasing
gentle showers of rain. Many precious bone relics were found and
devoted followers experienced wondrous visions. The second
Drubwang Pedma Rinpoche, Dzongnang Lama Kunzang Gyurmed
and many other great lamas built a gold and copper stupa, thirty
hand spans in height, to hold his precious relics. They also performed the ceremony of suppressing negative forces below the stupa's
base. Khenpo Sherab Zangpo of Mugsang and the second Drubwang Pedma Rinpoche performed the consecration rite for the
stupa, which was built to the left of the *Avalokiteshvara* temple.
Each year thereafter, many monks would congregate to perform
the one month long three *kaya* accomplishment ceremony to
commemorate the anniversary of Do-ngag Chökyi Nyima's
enlightenment, during which, on this auspicious occasion, many offerings are made.

This concludes the life story of the eighth throne holder of the
Palyul monastery and tradition, the third Karma Kuchen Rinpoche,
Orgyen Do-Ngag Chökyi Nyima.

This garden of Buddha's Doctrine of Sutra and Tantra
Is beautified by the sun of the Dharma,
With thousands of light rays of scholarship and accomplishment
Shining completely victorious in the sphere of space.

Do	Ngag	Chökyi	Nyima
Sutra	Tantra	Sun of	Dharma

Dharma Sun of *Sutra* and *Tantra*

13 The Second Drubwang Pedma Norbu Rinpoche, Pedma Kunzang Tendzin Norbu

The Ninth Throne Holder

One night, Do-ngag Chökyi Nyima dreamed that he was in his own residence, on the middle level of the temple containing the stupas that encase the remains of great lamas. Suddenly, a lama appeared who looked just like Dzongnang Lama, Kunzang Gyurmed, who said, "Oh look, Pedma Norbu is up there." Looking up, Do-ngag Chökyi Nyima saw the first Pedma Norbu seated behind one of the stupa windows with very white hair. When Do-ngag Chökyi Nyima approached, Pedma Norbu turned into a small child. The child that he saw in this dream and the young incarnation of the second Drubwang Pedma Norbu were identical. Before leaving this world, the first Pedma Norbu had prophesied, "When berries bloom again on the juniper tree next to my residence, my incarnation will come again to Palyul." A few years had already passed since the juniper tree began to produce berries.[1] Jamgon Khomtrul and many other great lamas of the time agreed that the correct incarnation had been found.

Khenpo Ngaga Rinpoche said that in Drubwang Pedma Norbu's past lifetimes he had been *Vajrapani;* the dharma master, Gar Dampa; the king's son, Damdzin Lhaje; Lhalung Palgyi Dorje; Tertön Sangye Lingpa, the first Drubwang Pedma Norbu; Dodrub Kunzang Shenphen, the first Drubchen Rinpoche; and Phuntsog Jungney, the second Drubchen Rinpoche.

Born in 1887, the fifteenth *rabjung* year of the Fire Pig, Pedma Norbu was brought to the Palyul monastery at the age of seven. When he was nine he had a direct vision of Padmasambhava and received blessings from him. He took novice ordination from Do-ngag Chökyi Nyima and was then given the name Pedma Kunzang Tendzin Norbu. In addition, from Do-ngag Chökyi Nyima, he received the empowerments and transmissions of Tertön Ratna Lingpa's revelations and the *Nam Chö* transmissions many times; the *Lama Gongdu* (Condensed Enlightened Mind of the Lama); *Kagyed* (Eight *Herukas*); Tertön Jatsön Nyingpo's revelations; Karma Lingpa's peaceful-wrathful *sadhanas;* the Kham and central Tibetan traditions of the *Dupa Do* (*Anu Yoga* empowerments and transmission); the entire Nyingma *Kama;* and essentially every single transmission practiced in the Palyul tradition.

From Palpung Lama Tashi Chöphel, he received the precious *Kagyur* transmission. Together with Palpung Kyabgon Situ Rinpoche, he received from Khenpo Gyaltsen Odzer, the entire *Rinchen Ter Dzöd* (Precious Terma Treasury) transmissions. Traveling to the glorious Kathog monastery, he received from Khenpo Kunpal Rinpoche (a direct disciple of Patrul Rinpoche) and Khenpo Ngaga Rinpoche, nearly one hundred volumes of teachings on the *sutras* and *tantras.* Through the process of mental examination and contemplation, Pedma Norbu ascertained the meaning of all that he learned. From Kathog Situ Rinpoche, Chökyi Gyatso, he received the empowerments and transmissions for the *Dam Ngag Dzöd* (Treasury of Essential Instructions) and many of the old, rare *terma* revelations. In particular, from his own extraordinary root guru, Khenpo Ngawang Palzangpo (Ngaga), he received full ordination in the lineage of Shantarakshita and the dharma name, Thubten Chökyi Langpo (Elephant of the Dharma of the Buddha's Doctrine). After ordination, the second Pedma Norbu Rinpoche practiced according to the *vinaya* and guarded his vows of what to accept and reject as carefully as he guarded his own eyes. When Khenpo Ngaga gave him secret oral teachings on the Great Perfection, his realization reached the pinnacle of the supreme Vajra Vehicle. He not only intellectually understood the profound teachings he received, he actualized awareness of the originally pure, naked and empty primordial nature. It was at this time that Pedma Norbu clearly displayed the signs of one who had realized the ever increasing visions of clear light *togyal.* Then, once again from the Vidyadhara Drodul Pawo Dorje, the second Pedma Norbu received the profound *Longchen Nyingthig* transmissions and teachings, which further enhanced his realization. Pedma Norbu, in return, offered Drodul Pawo Dorje the empowerments of *Kagyed* (Eight

Herukas); *Gongdu* Condensed Enlightened Mind); and the *Dupa Do Wang (Anu Yoga* empowerment) of the Kham tradition.

When Pedma Norbu Rinpoche was eighteen years of age, he traveled with Do-ngag Chökyi Nyima to the white rock of Gyaphu to meet the omniscient Mipham Rinpoche. Mipham Rinpoche transmitted all empowerments by using only one object, an image of *Manjusri*, as the Primordial Wisdom Being. With this sacred statue, Mipham Rinpoche blessed their minds giving the *Jampal Shiwa* (Peaceful *Manjusri*) and *Tragpo Tsedag* (Wrathful *Manjusri* Owner of Life) empowerments. Before his departure, Mipham Rinpoche told Pedma Norbu that if he studied with diligence, his life would be of great benefit to the Nyingmapa Doctrine.

The second Pedma Norbu then traveled to the Palpung Retreat Center to meet the great Jamgon Khomtrul Rinpoche. Pedma Norbu received Tertön Chög-gyur Lingpa's *Thugdrub* (Mind Accomplishment) empowerment from Jamgon Khomtrul, as well as many oral instructions on how to give empowerments and commentaries simultaneously. He predicted that Pedma Norbu would propagate the dharma by giving many empowerments, transmissions and teachings and he encouraged him to do so.

When Pedma Norbu was in his twentieth year, the third Karma Kuchen Rinpoche, Do-ngag Chökyi Nyima, left this world. Pedma Norbu was filled with sorrow at the passing of his precious guru. He felt especially great remorse because he had not received the great *Kagyed Desheg Dupa* (Eight *Herukas*-Essence of the *Sugatas*) transmission. Due to the impression that the intensity of this remorse made upon his mind, Do-ngag Chökyi Nyima came to him one night in a dream. For three consecutive days, Pedma Norbu received, while in the dream state, the entire transmission of the *Kagyed Desheg Dupa*. Prior to this dream, Pedma Norbu's reading ability was considered average. Following this experience, Pedma Norbu told the author, Tsering Lama, that he had suddenly acquired the ability to speed read.

After this transmission occurred in the dream state, it was acknowledged that Pedma Norbu had received the lineage directly from Do-ngag Chökyi Nyima. However, he also received the empowerment on another occasion from the vajra master, Shathang Lama Tseten. Kathog Situ Rinpoche said that Do-ngag Chökyi Nyima had transmitted the empowerment directly from the primordial wisdom mind to his heart disciple, Pedma Norbu.

When many disciples gathered together from all directions, Pedma Norbu would give the *Nam Chö* Great Perfection transmissions and the *Longchen Nyingthig* transmissions of Lama Lungtog's tradition, according to Khenpo Ngaga's oral instructions. Many of his own disciples became holders of these lineages. Throughout the days and nights that followed, Pedma Norbu persevered in the bestowal of transmissions to fortunate disciples. He continually gave all the empowerments, transmissions and commentaries of the *Nam Chö* revelations; Tertön Ratna Lingpa's revelations, *Kagyed, Gongdu* and *Dudo*. In addition, he often performed the great accomplishment ceremony of *Vajrasattva*. It was during this time, just prior to the concluding section of receiving the spiritual attainments, that Pedma Norbu had a dream while in a lucid state, in which Khenpo Gyaltsen Odzer gave him a gong containing five conch shells. Pedma Norbu instantly interpreted the dream to mean that his original empowering lama, Khenpo Gyaltsen Odzer, had given him permission to give the *Rinchen Ter Dzöd* (Precious Terma Treasury) empowerments five times during his life. Following this, he gave the *Rinchen Ter Dzöd* empowerments for the first time at Gojo Kyedpo monastery and Khantrul Rinpoche gave the transmission. Pedma Norbu gave the *Rinchen Ter Dzöd* empowerments for the second time at Gojo Gyara monastery and Mugsang Lama Kunzang Paljor gave the transmission.

The third great bestowal occurred in the year of the Earth Sheep at his own Palyul monastery when he gave the empowerments and transmissions to the second Chögtrul Rinpoche, the fourth Karma Kuchen Rinpoche and a large assembly of monks. The fourth bestowal occurred at the Dago retreat center and the fifth and final time, Pedma Norbu gave the empowerments to Khenpo Ngaga Rinpoche, completing all of the Khenpo's transmissions. At the conclusion of the fifth transmission, he said the omen dream of the five conch shells had been fulfilled.

From childhood, Pedma Norbu studied the science of medicine with Doctor Döndrub of Ney-gyab. He also learned the entire Sanskrit grammar book *Kalapa* and literature from Palpung Drangnyin Tsewang. From Gelong Getsa Khenrab Odzer of Kathog, he learned white and black astrology and the Indian and Chinese art of placement (geomancy). He studied poetry with Lama Sonam Tseten and wrote poetry using the inspiring omniscient Jigme Lingpa as his principal subject of praise. From Lama Shathang

Tseten, Dila Do-ngag Tendar and others, he studied mandala construction and chanting according to the Palyul tradition. Pedma Norbu wrote a new book on the subject of chanting and commissioned a wood block to be carved. From Lama Mongphen, the head chanter of Kathog, Lama Dragchog, the head chanter of Gyokhar, and Lama Kunzang Thutob, the head chanter of Bragnag, Pedma Norbu studied the central Tibetan and Kham traditions of the Mindroling system of chanting and ritual. Pedma Norbu himself became an unmatched scholar in mandala construction and the art of chanting. He always insisted that his disciples undergo the same training.

Pedma Norbu gave continual teachings on the *Sang Nying* (Secret Essence); *Yonten Dzöd* (Treasury of Pure Qualities); and *Dom Sum* (Three Vows). When large numbers of disciples gathered together, he gave extensive preliminary practice teachings throughout the day and night. Whatever subject he was teaching, he taught with great enthusiasm and without personal concern. In addition, he taught whatever was requested of him so as not to upset anyone. He even taught simple reading and writing and the common sciences of grammar, poetry, astrology and so forth; each many times. When disciples were slow to learn, he always pointed out and praised their potential.

It occurred that through the force of the fire element, the entire Dago monastery was burned to the ground. Together with Garwang Tendzin, Pedma Norbu sponsored the rebuilding of the main temple, the protector's temple, the lama's residence and the monastic compound. He commissioned the carving of many new wood blocks of the *Nyingthig Termas*, Khenpo Ngaga's Collected Works, the most important recitations and others. He had the Five Great Treasures of Kongtrul Rinpoche and a large amount of other precious scriptures rewritten, reprinted and restored.

A prophecy from Tertön Sangngag Lingpa states, "In the Palyul tradition of accomplishment, a scholastic college will be born to propagate the *sutras* and *tantras* in a way that is unprecedented." In 1922, the fifteenth *rabjung* year of the Water Dog, Pedma Norbu opened the new scholastic college in the Palyul monastery. When the college opened, fifty new students enrolled to begin the traditional study of the most important texts in the *sutras* and *tantras*. Pedma Norbu provided each one of them with every necessity.

Pedma Norbu built the new monastery of Gojo Banag where the

Nyingthig tradition was practiced exclusively and Khanang Tulku
Shedrub Gyatso of Pewar (an emanation of Tashi Phuntsog), was
appointed to take charge. He was a very pure, disciplined monk,
who had received signs of accomplishment in the root-recitation of
a great number of deities of the Three Roots. At Namdrag
monastery, during the great recitation of the Eight *Herukas Sadhanas*,
Shedrub Gyatso actually perceived the naked, empty nature of pure-
awareness. The second Pedma Norbu told him he had been introduced to the nature of the mind and had purely recognized that introduction. From that time onward, Shedrub Gyatso took the Eight
Herukas and Wrathful *Manjusri* Owner of Life as his extraordinary
meditational deities. Achieving great powers through these practices, he became known as Khang-nang Dredul (demon-subduer
from Khang-nang). In Gojo, Samdrub Shung, Pedma Norbu's
main disciple, Khenpo Karma Tashi, built a new retreat center
according to his guru's wishes. In this center, he opened a scholastic college and an accomplishment college in which only a
few top quality, fully ordained monks practiced the *Nyingthig* tradition exclusively. Later, Khenpo Karma Tashi asked Tulku Ajam
(younger brother of the third Pedma Rinpoche) to take charge of
this monastery.

At Dago retreat center, the second Drubwang Pedma Norbu
began the ten day great accomplishment ceremony of *Palchen Dupa*
(Padmasambhava), according to the *Nyingthig* tradition. During this
time, four *sadhanas* were simultaneously accomplished. These four
are: *Shinje Tsedag* (Wrathful *Manjusri* Owner of Life); *Tamtrin Kham
Sum Rolpa* (*Hayagriva*, Delighting in the Three Realms); *Yangdag
Sangye Nyam Jor* (*Yangdag* Buddha Union); and *Phurba Dudpung Zilnon*
(*Vajrakilaya* Suppression of an Army of Demons). These practices include a five part offering ceremony performed according to the Mindroling tradition. Pedma Norbu also wrote an extensive new index for this great accomplishment ceremony. In that
same year, he began the seven day *Avalokiteshvara* accomplishment
ceremony called *Dugngal Rangdrol* (Self-Liberation of Suffering); the three day *Nyingthig* accomplishment ceremony, *Gyutrul Shi-
drag* (Peaceful-Wrathful Illusory Manifestations); *Guru Puja*, called
Pagmed Nyurlam (Boundless Swift Path); and *Shi-tro Ngensong Jongwa*
(Peaceful-Wrathful Cleansing the Lower Realms). Pedma Norbu
provided the funds for all of these accomplishment ceremonies. He
compiled an extensive revised edition of the protectors and other

general prayers to be recited six times annually. He began the annual winter solstice and end of the old year practices of *Kagyed Desheg Duchen* (Eight *Herukas*-Great Assembly of *Sugatas*); *Jangter Tsedag* (Northern Treasure, Owner of Life); *Tro-wo* (Wrathful Deity); *Keng Kong* (Wrathful Deity); *Duddul Phurba* (Duddul's *Vajrakilaya*); *Yumka Sengdong* (Female Aspect Lion-faced Deity); and *Rolpa Chenpo Tordog* (Great Utilization of the *Torma* Reversal). On the auspicious tenth and twenty-fifth days of the lunar month, he instituted the practices of *Rigdu* (Padmasambhava of the *Nyingthig* tradition); *Yumka* (*Nyingthig* Dechen Gyalmo) and the *Nyingthig* Dharma Protectors. At Dago Monastery, practically all of the traditional practices that Pedma Norbu instituted were of the *Nyingthig* tradition.

In the village areas around the Palyul monastery, Pedma Norbu built many small temples, providing them with the three supports of the doctrine so that the local laymen and women could congregate and practice. At Ragchab monastery, he built a new temple with a golden central image of Buddha Shakyamuni, surrounded by the sixteen *Arhats* depicted in mountain settings.

The second Drubwang Pedma Norbu's commentaries and revised personal works on the *sutras* and *tantras* are compiled in seven large volumes. Later in his life, when he was not bestowing specific empowerments, transmissions, and teaching, or presiding over important accomplishment ceremonies, Pedma Norbu remained in solitary retreat, practicing the root recitation mantra of *Dugngal Rangdrol* (Self Liberation of Suffering) for three years, from the beginning of the year of the Iron Dragon until the year of the Iron Sheep. When the retreat concluded, he returned to the Palyul monastery to preside over the dharma medicine accomplishment of the Eight *Herukas*, practiced according to the Mindroling tradition.

That autumn, it seemed as though Pedma Norbu was attempting to abandon all of his worldly possessions when he sponsored the *Palchen Dupa* (Padmasambhava) accomplishment ceremony at Dago monastery. At the same time, he sponsored four hundred monks to perform the annual great accomplishment ceremony of *Vajrasattva*, according to the Mindroling tradition. Afterwards, he made boundless material offerings to accumulate great virtue. Literally abandoning everything, he entered into retreat at the isolated place of Khachu Trag. It was then that he began to show signs of physical illness.

Wishing to see Khenpo Ngaga Rinpoche, Pedma Norbu was carried on a palanquin to Khenpo Ngaga's monastery in Nyushul. It was at that time that Khenpo Ngaga Rinpoche was known to have said, "Since the passing of Situ Chökyi Jungney, the second Drubwang Pedma Norbu is the most important lama alive today who can bring great benefit to the Nyingmapa Doctrine." Khenpo Ngaga had many long life ceremonies performed for Pedma Norbu, but to no avail. When Khenpo Ngaga was away at Dralag monastery, Pedma Norbu's condition grew worse. One day, while the Khenpo was thinking of Pedma Norbu, they met one another in pure vision. Khenpo Ngaga asked about his health and several other questions. Pedma Norbu answered that he was ready to travel to the pure realms without any difficulty. The only regret he had was that he wished there was more time to serve the Great Perfection clear light tradition of the *Longchen Nyingthig* and more time to study under Khenpo Ngaga. Pedma Norbu then promised to quickly reincarnate.

In 1932, the sixteenth *rabjung* year of the Water Monkey, on the third day of the third month, the second Drubwang Pedma Norbu's mind entered the foundational sphere of truth. He was only forty-six years old. Khenpo Ngaga made many prayers for his swift rebirth and after some time had passed, he awakened Pedma Norbu from meditative absorption. For three consecutive days, the Khenpo made boundless offerings to his holy body in preparation for cremation. During the cremation, Khenpo Ngaga was joined by the fourth Karma Kuchen Rinpoche, Gyalsei Gyurmed Dorje, Kalzang Tenzin, and many other great lamas and monks. As Pedma Norbu's body was cremated, the *Tsogchen Dupa* (*Anu Yoga* Condensed Great Assembly) and *Kagyed Desheg Dupa* (Eight *Herukas* Condensed Essence of the *Sugatas*) practices were performed in four great mandalas. During this time, there was an earthquake, the sounds of countless self-originating dharma instruments reverberating throughout space, a wondrously sweet smell prevailing in all directions, circular rainbows filling the sky and other miraculous signs which filled the hearts of many of his disciples with renewed faith and devotion. At the mother Palyul monastery, all the monks performed offering ceremonies and built a large golden stupa, one story high, to stand next to the main temple to contain the second Drubwang Pedma Norbu's precious relics.

This concludes the life story of the ninth throne holder of the

Palyul monastery and tradition, the second Drubwang Pedma Norbu Rinpoche, Chökyi Langpo.

The greatness of the Dharma of kama and terma
Is upheld by the strength of the great royal elephant of dharma.
How marvelous is the appearance of this royal elephant
(the second Pedma Norbu)
To beautify and enrich the impartial garden
Of the Buddha's Doctrine.

Chökyi   Langpo
Dharma of   Royal Elephant

Royal Elephant of Dharma

14 The Fourth Karma Kuchen Rinpoche Thegchog Nyingpo
The Tenth Throne Holder

Thegchog Nyingpo was born in 1908, the fifteenth *rabjung* year of the Earth Monkey. His father was Tertön Rinchen Lingpa and his mother was Ah Pal, the daughter of Drodul Lama Azom Drugpa. The fifteenth Karmapa Khakyab Dorje prophesied that this child was indeed the reincarnation of the third Karma Kuchen Rinpoche Do-ngag Chökyi Nyima and gave him the name Karma Thegchog Nyingpo Drimed Yong Drub, which means the Stainless Fully Accomplished Essence of the Supreme Vehicle. The fifteenth Karmapa also composed his long life prayer. Drodul Lama Azom Drugpa also recognized the child, who was then brought to the Palyul monastery and enthroned as the tenth lineage holder of this Palyul tradition.

Thegchog Nyingpo received his first vows of refuge from Thubten Chökyi Langpo, the second Pedma Norbu. Thegchog Nyingpo invited the Dzogchen Khenpo Rigdzin Odzer to the Palyul monastery to give many teachings on the major volumes of *sutra* and *tantra*. From Jamgon Tai Situ Pedma Wangchog Gyalpo, Thegchog Nyingpo received full ordination and the name Karma Do Ngag Shedub Tenpai Nyima (Sun of the Doctrine of Teaching and Practice of the *Sutras* and *Tantras*). His character was naturally pure, like gold, and he upheld supreme moral discipline. From the second Drubwang Pedma Rinpoche and the Vidyadhara Drodul Lama (Azom Drugpa) he received profound teachings on the clear light Great Perfection. He received essential instructions on clearing obstacles and increasing advantageous conditions from the precious *Bodhisattva* Gyurmed Dorje. Through the strength of his precious guru's blessings and the residual karma from past training, with directionless mind, all his perceptions confidently relaxed into the great, all-pervasive *Dharmakaya*.

During his life, the author of this book had the opportunity to travel with the fourth Karma Kuchen Rinpoche, Karma Thegchog Nyingpo, to the congested city of Beijing, China. In such a distracting, crowded environment, Karma Thegchog Nyingpo was unaffected, maintaining the pure awareness of the profound expanse of the sphere of truth, experiencing the equal taste of *samsara* and *nirvana*. Witnessing the strength of this great master's realization, the author's faith and devotion was deeply intensified.

From the second Drubwang Pedma Rinpoche, Thegchog Nyingpo received the *Du Do (Anu Yoga)* empowerment, according to the *Dorje Them-Ke* Empowerment Text, and the *Dorje Drag Kham* tradition of the *Du Do (Anu Yoga* Empowerment), according to the text *Kilkor Gyatso Jugdog*. From Kathog Khenpo Legshed Jordan, Thegchog Nyingpo received the supreme empowerment *Drangtsi Chö Gyun* (A Continual Flow of Nectar) written by Mogton Dorje Palzang, making him a lineage holder of the earlier Kathog tradition. Also, from Khenpo Legshed, he received the entire teachings on the *Dam Ngag Dzöd* (Treasury of Essential Instruction). From the second Drubwang Pedma Rinpoche, he received the entire *Rinchen Ter Dzöd* empowerments, transmissions and teachings; the great empowerments of the *Lama Gongdu Accomplishment, Kagyed Drubwang* (Eight *Herukas* Accomplishment Empowerments); the *Sang Dzog Drubwang Bum Gyachen* (Great Empowerment-Perfected Secret-Sealed Vase) with simultaneous commentary and all the *Nam Chö* transmissions. In short, Thegchog Nyingpo received every important transmission in the Palyul lineage from the second Pedma Norbu, including minor transmissions for ritual practice, ransoming life, exorcism of negative forces and others. From the precious *Bodhisattva* Gyurmed Dorje, he received all the empowerments and transmissions of Rinchen Lingpa's revelations. The transmission of the *Nyingma Gyud Bum* was received from Palyul's senior *khenpo*, Jampal Dorje. After receiving all these transmissions, Thegchog Nyingpo entered into a three year retreat at the Palyul retreat center to practice Ratna Lingpa's Three *Kaya* Accomplishment.

After successfully completing the retreat, Thegchog Nyingpo began giving empowerments, transmissions and teachings to large gatherings. To the lamas and *tulkus* of Palyul, Gojo and disciples from all the surrounding areas, he gave the empowerments of Ratna

Lingpa's revelations as well as extensively teaching the *Nam Chö* and the peaceful-wrathful generation and completion stages three times. Most of the transmissions during this time were given by Kangnang Tulku and the second Dzongnang Rinpoche. In particular, Thegchog Nyingpo gave to the third Drubwang Pedma Rinpoche, Dzongnang Rinpoche, Drakmar Tulku Pedma Wangchen and a few others, the great *Gongdu Drubwang* (Empowerment of the Condensed Enlightened Mind Accomplishment), according to Jamgon Kongtrul Rinpoche's instruction manual. To the greater sangha community, he gave the central Tibetan tradition of the *Dupa Do Wang* (*Anu Yoga* empowerment). Thegchog Nyingpo commissioned the painting of ten *thankas* of the *Gongdu* meditational deities. He had many statues made, scriptures printed and stupas erected. He was always very generous toward the dharma and greater sangha community, accumulating an abundance of great merit.

In order to fully complete the miraculous activities of his predecessor, the fourth Karma Kuchen Rinpoche, Thegchog Nyingpo commissioned ten new volumes of the Golden Nyingma *Kama* to be written and printed. These volumes include the *Gyutrul Trakhor* (Subtle Illusory Manifestations Cycle); *Dodrel Monpai Gocha* (*Anu Yoga* Commentary on the Armor That Protects From Darkness); *Gegdor Parkab* (Gegdor's commentary to the Secret Essence called Par Kab); *Nyi-od Senge Gyacher Drol* (extensive commentary to the Secret Essence); and others. He made many improvements at the monastery by repairing the temple, building a new lama's residence, offering new materials to the three supports, making new lama dance costumes, umbrellas, canopies, banners and all the essential items. Thegchog Nyingpo traveled to Gojo three times and, during his third visit, he supplied all the monasteries in the area with the necessities to begin the annual *yarney* retreat. In addition, with the offerings he received, he had *thankas* painted of all the deities in the Nyingma *Kama*.

In 1950, the year of the Iron Tiger, Thechog Nyingpo began to build the new Namgyal Lhakang (Temple of Complete Victory) in order to benefit the doctrine. Unfortunately, he was able to complete only the temple's outer shell. In 1951, the year of the Iron Rabbit, he entered into a three year retreat to practice Tertön Ratna Lingpa's *Tse Sang* (Condensed Essence of *Amitayus*) and *Vajrakilaya's Nyinchen* (Great Root Recitation). In 1955, the year of the

Wood Sheep, Thegchog Nyingpo was invited to China to attend a special meeting for Tibetan spiritual leaders. While at this meeting, he assumed a position of authority in order to benefit the Buddha's doctrine. In 1956, the year of the Fire Monkey, the Communist Chinese occupation of Tibet began. During the fighting that followed, Thegchog Nyingpo went to Mugsang and received the precious *Kagyur* transmission from Khenpo Dam Chö Gyatso and while there, he performed the consecration ceremony for a new temple, a golden statue of Shakyamuni, a large statue of Padmasambhava and many other exquisitely crafted images, all built by Tulku Kunzang. The consecration ceremony he performed was the practice of engaging in the upper and lower activity through accomplishing *Vajrakilaya.*[1] During this visit, Thegchog Nyingpo also received the transmission of *Dorje Sempa Namkha* (*Vajrasattva* as Vast as Space) from Khenpo Khentsey Lodrö. In the year of the Fire Bird, after completing the wood block carving of the four volumes of the *Dodrel Chenmo* (Great Commentary to the *Anu Yoga*) he returned to the Palyul monastery.

In 1958, the year of the Earth Dog, Thegchog Nyingpo was fifty-one years old when he was captured and imprisoned by the Communist Chinese troops. After undergoing a great amount of torture, he was taken to the Mugngag Labor Camp. One day, Thegchog Nyingpo told his prison guards that he was planning to leave. Thinking he was planning an escape, the guards chided him saying, "We will see how far you get." They intended that evening to watch him very closely, but were distracted when a tigress with four cubs came near the prison. All of the guards on duty rushed off to hunt the tigress and what they found when they returned is told as follows: Some of the guards reported that Thegchog Nyingpo had completely disappeared, without leaving a trace behind (the great rainbow body transference), others said they found him sitting without breathing in meditative equipoise. The announcement was made to the general public that Thegchog Nyingpo had died suddenly of an unexplained illness.

This concludes the life story of the tenth throne holder of the Palyul monastery and tradition, the fourth Karma Kuchen Rinpoche, Thegchog Nyingpo Do-ngag Shedrup Tenpai Nyima.

This lotus garden of the teachings and practice
Of the sutras and tantras,
Is beautified by the sun of the doctrine,
Possessing thousands of light rays
Of scholarship and accomplishment,
Illuminating the space of the supreme, essential vehicle.

Do	Ngag	She	Drub	Tenpai	Nyima
Sutra	Tantra	Teaching	Practice	Doctrine	Sun

The Sun of the Doctrine of Teachings and Practices
of the *Sutras* and *Tantras*

15 The Third Drubwang Pedma Norbu Rinpoche, Thubten Lekshed Chokyi Drayang, also known as Do-ngag Shedrub Tendzin Chog-lei Namgyal
The Eleventh Throne Holder

The fifth Dzogchen Rinpoche, Thubten Chökyi Dorje, prophesied, "In a supreme and sacred place, in the upper region of
Puwo, close to an attractive, large, rocky mountain that is adorned
with various trees, surrounded by large and small lakes and a large
cold river flowing from the south, a child of noble birth will be
born in the year of the Water Monkey. His parents of method and
wisdom, will bear the names Sonam and Kyid. I have received in-
dications that this child will be of great benefit to the doctrine and
sentient beings." The great Khenpo Ngaga Rinpoche supported this
prophecy and recognized the new incarnation, composing his long
life prayer.

The third Drubwang Pedma Norbu was born in 1932, the year
of the Water Monkey, in the twelfth month. He was born in the
ancestral heritage of Terton Duddul Dorje. His father's name was
Sonam Gyurmed and his mother's name was Dzom Kyid. The third
Drubwang Pedma Norbu was invited to the Palyul monastery in
1936, the year of the Fire Rat, and took his vows of refuge from
the great Khenpo Ngaga Rinpoche.

One day at play, while still a small child, he accidentally broke
the horn on a very old and precious vajra. Fearing that his teacher
would reprimand him, Pedma Norbu quickly glued it back
together with his own saliva, making the vajra much stronger than

it had been originally. On another occasion, during the *Cha-sum* ceremony, he accidentally dropped his ritual bell onto the stone floor. Everyone present assumed that the bell had broken and yet, when Pedma Norbu picked it up, the ring was much more melodious than ever before. As a small child, the third Drubwang Pedma Norbu displayed many miraculous signs of accomplishment.

Pedma Norbu took *upasaka* (lay) ordination from the second Chögtrul Rinpoche and received the name Thubten Lekshed Chökyi Drayang (Doctrine Upholder of Eloquent Speech and Melodious Dharma). At Dago monastery, he received the *Nam Chö* Great Perfection one month preliminary practice teachings of Buddha in the Palm of the Hand and successfully completed all of the practices. The author of this book then taught him the general subjects of writing, poetry, astrology, medicine and so forth.

In 1944, the year of the Water Sheep, Pedma Norbu was twelve years old when he received the *Kagyed Do Wang Chenmo* (Great Empowerment of the Eight *Herukas*) and the *Rinchen Ter Dzöd* (Precious Terma Treasury) empowerments, transmissions and secret sealed protector empowerments from the second Chögtrul Rinpoche. From the fourth Karma Kuchen Rinpoche, Thegchog Nyingpo, he received *Nam Chö, Ratna Lingpa* and the *Kagyed Sang Dzog Drubwang Chenpo Bum Gya Chen* (Eight *Herukas* Accomplishment Empowerment of the Perfected Secret Sealed Vase) with simultaneous commentary. Also, from the fourth Karma Kuchen Rinpoche, he received, in twelve consecutive days, the *Gongdu Drubwang Chenmo* (Great Accomplishment Empowerment of the Condensed Enlightened Mind) according to Jamgon Rinpoche's Empowerment Index.

When Pedma Norbu was thirteen years of age, at the Dago retreat center, in front of the statue of Lord Buddha, situated in his predecessor's bedroom, he took novice ordination. During the ceremony, Khenpo Legshed Jordan was his *khenpo*, Khenpo Khentse Lodrö was his *sangtön* (secret teacher) and Tsamdo Khenpo Sonam Dondrub his helper. In addition, Khenpo Pedma Jigmed and several others were present to constitute the correct number of fully ordained monks present during an ordination ceremony.[1] During his ordination, the third Pedma Norbu received the name Do Ngag Shedrub Tendzin Chög-lei Namgyal, meaning Doctrine Upholder of the Teachings and Practices of *Sutra* and *Tantra* Victorious in all Directions. This lineage of ordination originated with Khenpo Shantarakshita, when he brought it to Tibet. From Khenpo Shantarakshita, the lineage has been gradually transmitted to the *Bodhisattva* Shenpen Tayey, who directly transmitted it to Lingtrul Gyaltsen Palzang, to the senior Kathog Lama Dorje Palzang, to Nyarong Khenpo Kalzang Wangchuk, to Kathog Situ Chökyi Gyatso, to the second Chögtrul Rinpoche, Thubten Do Ngag Chökyi Dawa and directly to the third Drubwang Pedma Norbu Rinpoche. Like a chain of golden mountains, this excellent lineage is unbroken and exceedingly pure.

Pedma Norbu received from Khenpo Legshed Jordan the Kham tradition of Mogton Dorje Palzang's Empowerment text *Wang Chög Drangtsi Chu Gyun* (A Continual Flow of Nectar) on two occasions, making him a holder of the earlier Kathog tradition. Khenpo Legshed Jordan also gave him all the empowerments, transmissions and teachings on the *Dam Ngag Dzöd* (Treasury of Essential Instruction); Tertön Dorje Lingpa's revelation *Lama Kadu* (Condensed Utterance of the Lama); *Hung Kor Nying Thig* (Hung Kor's Heart Essence); *Ngari Kagyed Yongdu* (Ngari's Completely Condensed Eight *Herukas*); Lerab Lingpa's revelation *Tendrel Ney Sel Kor* (Clarification of Negative Omens) and many others. From the fourth Karma Kuchen Rinpoche, Thegchog Nyingpo, Pedma Norbu received many transmissions, including the *Dupa Do Wang* (*Anu Yoga* empowerment) of the *Rinchen Trengwa* tradition, written by Nyalpa Deleg.

For forty-eight days in the forest above the Dago retreat center, Khenpo Lodrö performed the *Dupa Do (Anu Yoga)* accomplishment ceremony while giving the very first transmissions for his newly written four volumes. These transmissions were on Nubten's *Dodrel Munpai Gocha (Anu Yoga* Commentary, Armor Which Protects from Darkness), Dampa Rinpche's *Gog Bub* and Tsang Tönpa's word for word commentary on *Anu Yoga*. In attendance to receive the first auspicious transmissions were the third Drubwang Pedma Norbu, the second Dzongnang Rinpoche, Jampal Lodrö, Tulku Thubten Palzang, Shechen Khenpo Drayang and Palyul Khenpo Dondrub. The fact that there were five fortunate disciples present corresponds to the famous "gathering of the auspicious first five disciples" to receive new transmissions.[2]

Khenpo Khentse Lodrö noted that prior to the second Drubwang Pedma Norbu's passing he had given the Khenpo a small knife as a gift. At that time the khenpo wondered what was the significance of the gift, but now, he told the lamas, he realized it was the symbol of wisdom. He realized that this symbol was giving him the blessing to complete the composition of his new treatise so that they could be transmitted to Pedma Norbu's incarnation.

From Pedma Jigmed, the third Drubwang Pedma Norbu Rinpoche received the transmissions of Jigmed Lingpa's Nine Volumes; the thirteen chapters of Karma Chagmed's *Ah Chö* (Dharma-*Ah*); and So Wangdrag Gyatso's *Ka Bum* (Collected Works). While receiving these transmissions, Pedma Norbu made intricately woven knots in blessings cords with his tongue. He continued to make these wondrous special blessing cords until 1958.[3]

On another occasion, Pedma Norbu casually drew in ink the syllable *"Ah"* on a white conch shell. Later, when the ink wore away, the syllable was luminously embossed on the shell. This shell, cherished as an object of veneration, is presently kept in the Palyul monastery in Tibet. The third Pedma Norbu twice completed the full retreat of the Illusory Body of *Manjusri* (a Mind Treasure of Mipham Rinpoche). Just at the conclusion of the second retreat, a very melodious sound could be heard coming from his shrine room and a brilliant light radiated from the mirror on his altar.

In the Darthang monastery, Pedma Norbu received all the transmissions of the precious *Kagyur* and *Tengyur*, as well as completing a *Vajrakilaya* retreat. He then entered into retreat with his root guru, Chögtrul Rinpoche, for four consecutive years. During these four precious years that they remained together, Chögtrul Rinpoche, who was already quite elderly, suffered from extremely poor vision. It was with great personal difficulty and hardship that he gave the third Drubwang Pedma Norbu Rinpoche all the empowerments, transmissions and secret oral instructions of Tertön Migyur Dorje's *Nam Chö* (Space Treasures), Ratna Lingpa's revelations and virtually every single transmission practiced in the great Palyul tradition. Pedma Norbu Rinpoche then successfully completed all the stages of practice directly under Chögtrul Rinpoche's guidance. Among his accomplishments were the root recitations of the Three Roots *(Lama, Yidam, Khandro)*, the *Nam Chö* preliminary practices, *tummo-tsalung;* the actual foundation practices of the Great Perfection Buddha in the Palm of the Hand, which include *trekchöd,* clear light *togyal,* inner *togyal* practice, darkness practice, training in the dream state, the nature of sound and the pure realms. It was during this time that Chögtrul Rinpoche was known to have said, "If I am unable to successively transmit all empowerments, transmissions and teachings to the third Pedma Norbu Rinpoche before I leave this world, then my precious human rebirth will have been wasted." It has come to pass that the third Drubwang Pedma Rinpoche is the only great lama alive today who holds entirely the pure lineage of Tertön Migyur Dorje's *Nam Chö* and Ratna Lingpa's revelations.

When Pedma Norbu later returned to the Palyul monastery he had thirty new lama dance costumes made out of the very best Japanese silk brocade for the major lama dances performed there. With Khenpo Nuden, Khenpo Sonam Döndrub, Khenpo Dondrub and others, he studied the *sutras* and developed penetrating intelligence. Afterwards, he traveled on pilgrimage to central Tibet to visit the major spiritual centers of Samye, Dorje Drag, Mindroling, Drepung, Gaden, Sera, Lhasa and others. In all of these great centers, Pedma Norbu made many impartial offerings. Accumulating a great amount of virtue and merit, he returned to Palyul monastery in 1956, the year of the Fire Monkey. Pedma Norbu Rinpoche renovated the entire Dago monastery, which was located close to the mother monastery, and gave all the empowerments, transmissions and teachings of the Nam Chö and Ratna Lingpa's revelations twice to Lungtog Rinpoche, Khenpo Nuden and many other fortunate disciples.

In an attempt to reverse the onset of the Chinese occupation, Pedma Norbu selected monks from the Palyul Scholastic College, Retreat Centers and main monasteries to perform, in individual groups, an extensive one month *Vajrakilaya* accomplishment. In addition to the main *sadhana*, they performed the lower activity of reversal, suppression, annihilation of negative forces and the fire offering ceremony. During that same month, Pedma Norbu simultaneously began the practice of *Magon Yul Do* (the *Torma Reversal of Mahakala* and *Ekatsatri*) and the Long Life Accomplishments. He sponsored a total of two hundred monks to perform these important and timely practices. While these accomplishments were underway, various signs arose indicating that the Communist Chinese occupation of Tibet was irreversible. It was then that the third Drubwang Pedma Norbu Rinpoche made his decision to depart for India, leaving the Palyul monastery for the purpose of the doctrine and sentient beings. On the long, dangerous journey that followed, Pedma Norbu passed through central Tibet and crossed over the border into India. He was constantly befriended and safeguarded by the meditational deities and dharma protectors during this difficult journey.

Once in India, he began activating expansive miraculous activities and shortly after he decided to settle in Mysore, South India, close to the sacred *Drekar Pungwa Stupa*, where Buddha first taught the *Kalachakra Tantra*.

In 1963, the year of the Water Rabbit, Pedma Norbu Rinpoche built the new Thekchog Namdrol Shedrub Dargye Ling monastery (the Monastery That Propagates the Teachings and Practices of the Supreme Vehicle that Fully Liberates) and he established the sangha community.

At Namdroling monastery, the third Drubwang Pedma Norbu Rinpoche established the tradition of *yarney* (rainy season retreat); *gaye* (a special practice performed at the conclusion of *yarney* sojourn); Tertön Karma Lingpa's One Thousand Offerings to the Peaceful and Wrathful Deities; the *Vajrasattva* Accomplishment Offering Ceremony; Tertön Ratna Lingpa's *Vajrakilaya* (to expel negativities at the end of the old year); the Great Accomplishment of One Hundred Million Recitations, using different mandalas each year; the *Anu Yoga* offering accomplishment ceremony of the Great Gathering; the Great Dharma Medicine Accomplishment Ceremony; and many others.

During one of the Dharma Medicine Accomplishment Ceremonies of *Nyingthig Palchen Dupa* (Padmasambhava), rainbows arose from the mandala, the nectar in the skull cup overflowed and many other extraordinary signs of accomplishment were viewed by many. During the mantra recitation, Pedma Norbu Rinpoche suddenly experienced an extremely sweet taste in his mouth, which he later mentioned to Khenpo Namdrol. For the last twenty-six successive years since arriving in India, the third Drubwang Pedma Norbu has continued the annual tradition of performing the accomplishment of the one hundred million mantra repetitions.

On one auspicious day, a sign occurred to indicate that the Nyingma tradition of scholars would continue in this monastery. Pedma Norbu Rinpoche casually wrote in ink the root mantra of *Manjusri*, the *bodhisattva* of wisdom, upon a white conch shell. After the ink wore off, the mantra was luminously embossed on the conch.

Khenpo Namdrol and many other monks at the monastery witnessed this. On another occasion, when Pedma Norbu Rinpoche had to have a tooth extracted, his attendant Kunzang kept the tooth as an object of veneration and placed it in his amulet for safekeeping. Nine years later, when he again looked at the tooth, he was surprised to find that the tooth had given birth to two precious relics and that since that time another relic has self-originated.

Presently, all the major lineage-holding *tulkus* and lamas of the Palyul tradition are in residence at Namdroling monastery under the guidance of the third Drubwang Pedma Norbu. There are eighteen *tulkus*, ranging from eight to twenty-one years of age. Prominent among these are the most important reincarnate lineage holders of this tradition, such as the fifth Karma Kuchen Rinpoche, the third Chögtrul Rinpoche and the third Rago Chögtrul Rinpoche. The spiritual training that they receive is directly under Pedma Norbu Rinpoche's guidance, according to this pure tradition of accomplishment.

In 1977, Khenpo Tsundru was invited from Sikkim to come to Namdroling monastery and in 1978, on the seventeenth day of the second month, the new Scholastic College at Namdroling monastery was officially opened. The college received the name *Ngagyur Tolob Do Ngag Rigpai Jungney Ling* (the Nyingma College of Advanced Studies called the Source of Knowledge in *Sutra* and *Tantra*). The scholastic college presents a nine year study program that includes the in-depth study of fifty major scriptures of the Buddhist canon. These major works of the greatest Indian and Tibetan scholars of *sutra* and *tantra* are studied under a team of fully qualified *khenpos*. Over one hundred students, coming from Tibet, Bhutan, Sikkim, Nepal and India, are enrolled in the college. To date, the *khenpos* who have taught in the Scholastic College include Khenpo Tsundru, Khenpo Rinchen, Khenpo Dazer, Khenpo Pema Sherab, Khenpo Namdrol, Khenpo Rigzin, Khenpo Tseten and Khenpo Tsewang Gyatso. In addition, many of the graduating students are also qualified to become *khenpos* themselves. At the present, not only is this college of great benefit to the propagation of the Nyingmapa Doctrine, it is well known as the largest Nyingmapa Scholastic College in the world today.

In 1982, the third Drubwang Pedma Norbu returned to his homeland, Palyul, Tibet. While visiting the site of the mother Palyul monastery and branch monasteries, he made many generous

offerings to support the reconstruction of the temples and to pro-
vide for the needs of the gathering sangha community. Hundreds
and thousands of faithful gathered from all directions to receive the
empowerments, transmissions and teachings that he bestowed.
Endlessly and tirelessly, he fulfilled the requests of the people
throughout the day and night. During this visit, the third Drubwang Pedma Norbu presided over the great and precious Dharma
Medicine Accomplishment and the ordination of over five hundred monks.

In 1983, he returned to India and printed and distributed hun-
dreds of copies of the newly acquired, complete *Nam Chö* and Ratna
Lingpa's revelations, as well as other important scriptures of the
Palyul tradition. In 1984, Pedma Norbu turned the wheel of em-
powerments, transmissions and teachings of Tertön Migyur Dorje's
Nam Chö revelations for the first time in the holy land of India.
Simultaneously, he gave all the empowerments and transmissions of
Tertön Ratna Lingpa's revelations. These profound transmissions
were received by the fifth Karma Kuchen Rinpoche, the third
Chögtrul Rinpoche, Venerable Tulku Thubten Palzang, many *tulkus*,
khenpos, monks and over two thousand lay people. Once again, Pedma Norbu began to teach the precious and rare *Nam Chö* tradition of
the one month preliminary practice retreat, forty-four day *tummo tsa-
lung* practice, clear light *togyal*, and so forth.

In keeping with the tradition of his predecessors, in 1985 Pedma
Norbu opened the traditional three year retreat center at Namdroling monastery. According to this tradition of accomplishment,
while in retreat, each practitioner must perform the root-recitation
accomplishment practices of the Three Roots, the profound Great
Perfection practice of *trekchöd* and the inner-most secret accomplishments.

In that same year, at the request of Palyul Gyatrul Rinpoche, the
third Pedma Norbu Rinpoche turned the wheel of empowerments
of the *Nam Chö* revelations for the first time in the west when the empowerments and commentaries were given at Tashi Chöling, the
retreat center for Yeshe Nyingpo, located in the mountains, near
the border of California and Oregon, in the United States of
America. The empowerments were given daily for one month and
simultaneously translated into English. Tibetan *tulkus*, lamas and
monks attended, as well as over one hundred American lay-
Buddhist disciples. Many astonishing signs of accomplishment oc-

curred during this historic time.

In 1986, at the request of Rigo Tulku, the third Drubwang Pedma Norbu once again gave the empowerments of the *Nam Chö* revelations at Palyul Chökhor Ling, in North India. Many high lineage-holding *tulkus*, including Minling Dungsei, Minling Khen Rinpoche, Rigo Tulku, Rago Tulku, Kidpo Tulku, Dragmar Tulku, as well as two thousand lamas, monks and lay people attended.

The third Drubwang Pedma Norbu Rinpoche continually satisfies the needs and desires of his people by performing ceremonies to stop or create rain, to transfer the consciousness of the dead and dying, as well as after-death intermediate period ceremonies, exorcisms, long life blessings, healings, and so forth. There is no limit to the extent of his selfless, enlightened activities and powerful miraculous deeds. His efforts for the doctrine and sentient beings are equal only to the limits of space.

It was this author's great merit and fortune to be able to directly meet this great, living Buddha and to hear his nectar-like speech and in particular, to remain together with him as one mandala during the great Dharma Medicine Accomplishment Ceremony, which was recently held again in the snow land of Tibet. The prayer is offered that Pedma Norbu Rinpoche may live for hundreds and thousands of aeons, placing his lotus feet firmly in this world. With great faith and respect in the indivisible nature of the three secrets,[4] this heartfelt prayer is made.

This concludes a brief account of part of the life of the eleventh throne holder of the Palyul monastery and tradition, the third Drubwang Pedma Norbu Rinpoche. There is no doubt that his enlightened activities will continue to illuminate the darkness of ignorance in this world and that there will be the good fortune to continue to document his historical works for the benefit of the Buddha's doctrine and all sentient beings.

The peak of the great mountain of the Buddha's Doctrine,
Blazes with the brilliant halo of the sun and moon
Of the sutras and tantras.
Together with the eloquent melody of dharma speech
The blessings prevail throughout all the realms of this world!

Thubten	Do	Ngag	Leg	Shad
Buddha's Doctrine	Sutra	Tantra	Eloquent	Speech

Chökyi	Drayang
Dharma	Melodious Sound

The Eloquent Melodious Sound of Dharma Speech
of the Buddha's Doctrine

16 Other Important Palyul Lamas

The following is an acknowledgement of the lives of several great lamas who were extremely kind and important to the Palyul lineage.

Wangchug Tulku Rigzin Jigmed Rangdrol

Although he was not a throne holder of the Palyul lineage, Wangchug Tulku Rigzin Jigmed Rangdrol (the nephew of Karma Tashi) was an important lineage-holding lama of the Palyul tradition . Born in 1820, the fourteenth *rabjung* year of the Iron Dragon, he lived during the time of the seventh throne holder, Gyatrul Rinpoche.

Wangchug Tulku took vows of full ordination from Tai Situ Pedma Nyinched Wangpo and received the name Karma Tendzin Chökyi Gyalpo. He received, from Karma Gyurmed, all the transmissions of the golden Palyul tradition and, from Jigmed Gyalwai Ngu-gu, all of the profound *Longchen Nyingthig* transmissions. From the great Kathog Lama, Gyurmed Tsewang Chögdrub, he received extensive empowerments, transmissions and essential oral insructions from both lineages of *kama* and *terma*. During the earlier part of his life, Wangchuk Tulku assumed responsibility for the Palyul monastery and the great strength of his activities greatly uplifted the doctrine. Later, Wangchug Tulku went to Mugsang and entered into retreat in the *dagam wang pug* (half-moon power cave). At Tsangshe Dorje Drolod, he fully accomplished all the innermost essential practices. Impartially, he cared for many fortunate disciples, giving all the necessary transmissions and teachings to fulfill their needs. In Mugsang, he built a new temple to contain a golden stupa which was one story high, as well as three hundred bronze and gold statues. Due to his strength in the generation and completion stage practices, the dharma protectors became Wangchuk Tulku's servants. He practiced and taught the *Bodhicharya Avatara* (*Bodhisttva's* Way of Life) and *Abidharma Kosha* (Treasury of Actualization of Dharmas), making it a tradition of oral transmission at the monastery which continues to the present day. As an accomplished adept, Wangchuk Tulku had the power to tame the minds of all form and formless beings.

His reincarnation, Pedma Kunzang Tenzin, was born to a minister of the Dege king, in the Gyang Khang family. As a child, Pedma Kunzang Tenzin lived in Mugsang and received empowerments, transmissions and teachings from many great lamas, such as Jamyang Khentsey Wangpo, Jamgon Lodrö Thaye, Rigzin Drodul Pawo Dorje, Gyatrul Rinpoche, and others. Although there was much expectation that Pedma Kunzang Tenzin would become a great upholder of the doctrine, towards the latter part of his life he became involved in the political administration of the Dege government, which limited his direct involvement in dharma activities.

Pedma Garwang Tendzin

Pedma Garwang Tendzin, better known as Lhatrul Rinpoche, was the direct incarnation of Asam (Karma Tashi's nephew) and the body, speech and mind emanation of Karma Gyurmed. Pedma Garwang Tendzin was born in the fourteenth *rabjung* year of the Water Dog, in the area of Wontön Lhadrang. He was recognized, obtained and ordained by Gyatrul Rinpoche. He received every transmission in the Palyul tradition of accomplishment many times over and, as an exceedingly honorable monk, Pedma Garwang Tendzin upheld the *vinaya* discipline impeccably. He built a new temple at Dagor and commissioned the well-known artist of Chamdo, Kar Shod, to paint in gold, one thousand fresco images of Buddha. The temple's main image was Buddha Shakyamuni, standing one story high. He made a thorough study of the important root *Tantras, Gyud Sangwai Nyingpo* (Secret Essence of *Tantra*) and the *Dom Sum Nam-Ngei* (Certainty of the Three Vows). He had wood block prints made of the *Sangdag Gong-gyen* (*Vajrapani's* Ornament of the Enlightened Mind), *Chö-drag Chidon* (Chödrag's General Meaning) and *Domdrel Pagsam Nyeima* (Commentary to the Three Vows—A Wishgranting Stalk).

When Gyatrul Rinpoche traveled to Golog to build the new Darthang monastery, Pedma Garwang Tendzin accompanied him as
his attendant. He later was placed in charge of Darthang monastery
where he built a new retreat center, giving those who wished, the
opportunity to enter into the traditional three year retreat. In the
lower region of Golog, Pedma Garwang Tendzin built the new
Rongon Chöling monastery, housing three hundred monks. He
also recognized the new incarnation of Zigag Chögtrul Rinpoche
and arranged for him to stay at Darthang monastery, where he provided him with the best guidance and training, bestowing all
necessary empowerments and transmissions. Upon returning to
Palyul, Pedma Garwang Tendzin united the upper and lower
retreat centers and built better facilities. Thoroughly examining the
needs of each retreatant, he supplied them with every essential
item for practice. The barley crops from his own fields were offered to pay for the retreatants' expenses.

In 1925, the fifteenth *rabjung* year of the Wood Ox, Pedma Garwang Tendzin entered retreat to practice Guru Chöwang's *Yang
Nying Dupa* and to accomplish ten million recitations of the mantra
Om Mani Pedme Hung. After successfully completing the retreat, he
returned to Darthang monastery and entered into another very
strict retreat where he remained until his eighty-fourth year.

It was in 1945, the sixteenth *rabjung* year of the Wood Bird, that
Pedma Garwang Tendzin's miraculous activities of this life were
completed and he dissolved his *Rupakaya* form body. His incarnation, Lhundrub Gyatso, was born into the same family heritage as
his predecessor. At the age of five, he was brought to Palyul
monastery, enthroned and given the *Rinchen Ter Dzöd* (Precious Terma Treasury) empowerments and transmissions from Chögtrul Rinpoche. He later accompanied Chögtrul Rinpoche on his journey to
Lhasa. Although Lhundrub Gyatso was destined to become a great
lineage holder, when he returned home from the journey to Lhasa,
he became ill and left this world at a very young age. His present
incarnation is residing at Darthang monastery in Tibet and it is said
that his miraculous activities are expansive and greatly beneficial to
the doctrine.

The First Chögtrul Rinpoche

The first Chögtrul Rinpoche, Zitrul Jamyang Sherab Chökyi

Nangwa, was born in 1854, the fourteenth *rabjung* year of the Wood Tiger, in the Gyarong area of Zigag. He was the incarnation of Dzong-nang Lama, Karma Lhawang. Recognized by Gyatrul Rinpoche and the omniscient Jamgon Rinpoche, Chögtrul Rinpoche was enthroned at the Palyul monastery. From his own tradition of Palyul, he received the *kama*, *terma* and many countless empowerments and transmissions. In particular, from Gyatrul Rinpoche, he received teachings on the outer sciences of medicine, grammar and poetry, and the inner teachings on the *sutras* and *tantras*. With great perseverance, he developed extremely profound wisdom-knowledge in all subjects and became known as a great scholar. Chögtrul Rinpoche composed a well-known *Kunzang Khorlo*[1] (Wheel of Praise) honoring his guru, Gyatrul Rinpoche.

Although Chögtrul Rinpoche was an outstanding scholar and an important lineage holding lama, the merit of sentient beings was weak. At the age of forty, in 1893, the fifteenth *rabjung* year of the Water Snake, at Dzong Shod, where Jamgon Rinpoche was staying, Chögtrul Rinpoche passed beyond this world. His incarnation was the second Chögtrul Rinpoche, Chökyi Dawa, and a brief account of his life follows.

Pedma Thegchog Tendzin

Pedma Thegchog Tendzin was an incarnation of both Gyatrul Rinpoche's uncle, Lama Sangye Yeshe, and the *Mahasiddha* of Gyalkhaba, Sakyapa Kunga Lodrö. He was born in the family heritage of Gyang-Khang into the family line of one of the four great ministers of the Dege king. Recognized by Gyatrul Rinpoche, Pedma Thegchog Tendzin was enthroned in the Palyul monastery. As a disciple of both Gyatrul Rinpoche and the third Karma Kuchen Rinpoche, Do-ngag Chökyi Nyima, he received from both of them all the empowerments, transmissions and, in great detail, the commentaries of the *kama* and *terma*. Through his continual single-pointed perseverance in practice, he became a greatly realized *bodhisattva*. During the time of the Chinese takeover of Tibet, Pedma Thegchog Tendzin's activities for the benefit of the doctrine were completed and he passed from this world. His reincarnation, Konchog Tenpai Gyaltsen (Gyang-kang Tulku) was born in the family heritage of Lama Lungtog Rinpoche. Discovered by the second Drubwang Pedma Norbu Rinpoche and the omniscient Khenpo

Ngaga, he was obtained and brought to the Palyul monastery where the second Pedma Norbu Rinpoche taught him reading, writing and all the basics. When he studied the *Dom Sum Nam-Nge* and the *Bodhicharya Avatara* his understanding was exceptional. Whatever he put his mind to was easily understood, causing everyone to believe he would one day become a very great scholar. Unfortunately, he passed away as a youth, in the year of the Water Monkey.

Thubten Palzang

Konchog Tenpai Gyaltsen's incarnation was Thubten Palzang, born in the year of the Fire Rat, in the family heritage of the second Pedma Norbu Rinpoche. He was discovered by the great Khenpo Ngaga. He received the *Rinchen Ter Dzöd* (Precious *Terma* Treasury) from Chögtrul Rinpoche and the *Dam Ngag Dzöd* (Treasury of Essential Instruction), the *Do Wang Drangtsi Chu Gyun* (*Anu Yoga* Empowerment-Continual Flow of Nectar) from Khenpo Legshed Jordan. From Lungtog Chögtrul Rinpoche, he received all the *Longchen Nyingthig* empowerments and oral transmission teachings. From Khenpo Khentse Lodrö, he received the *Du Do Drelwa* (*Anu Yoga* Commentary) and many other empowerments and transmissions. Free from the stain of partiality, Thubten Palzang's activities are like a great ocean of enlightened conduct for the benefit of the doctrine and sentient beings. Thubten Palzang presently resides at and presides over the Palyul monastery in Tibet.

Ka Sherab Lama Netan Jampal Thaye

Ka Sherab Lama Netan Jampal Thaye was the principal disciple of Chökyi Nyima, the third Karma Kuchen Rinpoche. As an incarnation of Sherab Gyatso of Barkhyim, he had superior discipline and strong determination in practice. He was a dharma teaching assistant to Chökyi Nyima and received a great amount of empowerments, transmissions and teachings. As a lineage-holding lama, he gave empowerments and teachings to the second Drubwang Pedma Rinpoche and other great lamas, thus becoming their guru. At the time of his passing, rainbows and astonishing signs were witnessed, including a piece of his bone that would not burn during cremation. Ngaga Rinpoche said this was called the small rainbow body accomplishment. Bagom Lama of the expanse class lineage of the Great Perfection and many of his disciples achieved this small rainbow body accomplishment.

The Second Chögtrul Rinpoche

The second Chögtrul Rinpoche, Thubten Jigmed Shedrub Chökyi Dawa Jampal Gyepai Dorje, was born in 1894, the fifteenth *rabjung* year of the Wood Horse, into the family heritage of Kunzang Sherab. The second Chögtrul Rinpoche was an emanation of Zitrul Jamyang Sherab Chökyi Nangwa, who was an emanation of the fifth throne holder Karma Lhawang. Although formally recognized as Zitrul Chökyi Nangwa's incarnation, Jampa Chödzin, the Mahasiddha of Tsangkor, and others said he was definitely an incarnation of Gyatrul Rinpoche.

The second Chögtrul Rinpoche was enthroned as a child at the Palyul monastery. He received, from the third Karma Kuchen Rinpoche, every possible teaching and, from Garwang Tendzin, all of the mind ripening commentaries, empowerments and transmissions in his own Palyul tradition. He received many teachings on the *sutras* and *tantras* from Khewang Sonam Palden and Dodrub Khenpo Kamme. Chögtrul Rinpoche's diligence in study, coupled with his inherent intelligence, made him an unequalled and superb scholar. In a previous lifetime, he had been the head lama of Sera monastery, which is a major monastery in the Gelug tradition. Due to the ripening of habitual impressions from that lifetime, he was very fond of the Gelug tradition and always carried the collected works of Je Tsongkhapa, the founder of the Gelug order, with him wherever he went. In addition, he was never separated from the Seven Great Treasure Volumes of Longchenpa.

From Kathog Situ Chökyi Gyatso, Chögtrul Rinpoche received full ordination in the lineage of Shantirakshita and the name Thubten Jigmed Shedrub Chökyi Dawa Trinley Rabgye Palzangpo. He became a perfect upholder of the *vinaya* rules of conduct. In addition to ordination, Chögtrul Rinpoche received the *Gongdu* accomplishment empowerment from Kathog Situ Rinpoche. He received complete teachings on the Non-Dual Great Seal *Mahamudra*-Great Perfection *Ati Yoga*, the *Rinchen Ter Dzöd* (Precious *Terma* Treasury) empowerments and transmissions and the ocean-like transmissions of *kama* and *terma* from the second Pedma Norbu

Rinpoche, Chökyi Langpo. Whether traveling or remaining at his
own Darthang monastery, he always maintained his regular daily
practice schedule. The amount of root recitations and accomplishment practices of the Three Roots and *dharmapalas* of *kama* and
terma that he fully accomplished is beyond number. Although
Chögtrul Rinpoche received clear signs of accomplishment in all
practices, he took great care to conceal these signs from others.
Chögtrul Rinpoche visited Golog, Serthar and Gyarong on several
occasions to bestow major empowerments and transmissions on
countless devotees. Since most of the monasteries in those areas
had been damaged by war, Chögtrul Rinpoche worked to restore
them by providing financial and material assistance. The kindness
he showed to the Palyul tradition was boundless.

In the mother Palyul monastery, the three supports of the doctrine had been dismantled by bandits from Chagtreng, a region in
Kham. Chögtrul Rinpoche restored the mother monastery and built
a beautiful new gold and copper pagoda on the top of the Chagdra
Lhosar temple. He made many generous offerings, without any
partiality, to the greater sangha communities extending from Am-
do to Palyul.

The Chinese soldiers had damaged Darthang monastery so badly
that it was practically gutted. Chögtrul Rinpoche worked to fully
restore Darthang and then filled it with new images, the *Kagyur*,
Tengyur and hundreds of important scriptures. He built a new
golden temple and filled it with the three supports of the doctrine.
Restoring his own personal residence, Thongo Ladrang, he maintained that as his seat for the duration of his life.

Chögtrul Rinpoche began the traditional *yarney* (rainy season
retreat) with three hundred novice and fully-ordained monks.
Building a new scholastic college, he propagated the major
teachings of the *sutras* and *tantras*. In 1940, the year of the Iron
Dragon, he traveled to the Palyul monastery to receive from
Kathog Khenpo Legshed Jordan, the *Anu Yoga* empowerment,
Drangtsi Chu Gyun (Continual Flow of Nectar) and many other im-
portant empowerments.

In the year of the Iron Snake, Chögtrul Rinpoche traveled to Gojo to give empowerments and teachings in all the branch
monasteries and establish many profound spiritual connections.
While visiting Rago Chögtrul Rinpoche, they had pleasant conversations and exchanged empowerments. Following this, Chögtrul

Rinpoche traveled to central Tibet to visit the three great dharma centers of Samye, Lhasa and Tradrug, making boundless offerings in these holy power sites. He then visited Sera, Drepung, Ganden, Tashi Lhunpo, Tsurphu and the upper and lower *tantric* colleges, making generous offerings to all the sangha communities. After visiting all the major and minor centers of Nyingmapa practice, such as Dorje Trag, Mindroling and Palri Thekchog Ling, he returned to Palyul in 1943, the year of the Water Sheep. Upon his return he gave the great *Rinchen Ter Dzöd* (Precious *Terma* Treasury) empowerments to the present third Pedma Norbu Rinpoche; the two *tulkus* of Gochen; *tulkus* from the monasteries of Gojo; the *khenpos* of Kathog and Palyul and many monks. The transmissions for these empowerments were given by Palyul's Khenpo Lodrö. Following this, Chögtrul Rinpoche gave the *Nam Chö ngundro* (Preliminary Practice Teachings) to the third Drubwang Pedma Norbu, the second Dzongnang Chögtrul Jampal Lodrö and others. When Khenpo Legshed Jordan arrived, Chögtrul Rinpoche gave the *Rinchen Ter Dzöd's* innermost secret empowerments and transmissions, as well as the Medicine Deity *Kama* empowerment, according to Lama Nyoton's text. Chögtrul Rinpoche gave novitiate ordination to the third Pedma Norbu and full ordination to many others.

In 1944, the year of the Wood Monkey, he returned to his Darthang monastery to give the *Nam Chö* empowerments and transmissions, the teaching of the Great Perfection Buddha in the Palm of the Hand, clear light *togyal* and Ratna Lingpa's revelations to the third Pedma Norbu, to Dzongnang Rinpoche and others. After receiving the precious *Kagyur* transmission from Lama Pedma Jigmed, Chögtrul Rinpoche went to the sacred place of *Avalokiteshvara*, called Dungri, in Gyarong, and entered into solitary retreat.

In 1957, the year of the Fire Bird, two years before the Chinese troops took complete control of Darthang monastery, Chögtrul Rinpoche casually told many of his disciples that he felt it was no longer beneficial for him to remain in the world. Immediately, the *khenpos, tulkus* and many other monks gathered together to make formal requests to Chögtrul Rinpoche to remain longer. In addition, they performed many extensive long life ceremonies in his honor. Chögtrul Rinpoche then told his disciples they would have the opportunity to perform all the appropriate offering ceremonies if he passed away at this time, but since they insisted, he would live a few more years.

Two years went by and in 1959 the Chinese troops took over Darthang monastery and the surrounding areas, capturing and imprisoning Chögtrul Rinpoche at Chedri labor camp. They imprisoned many of Darthang's *khenpos, tulkus* and important monks. Several days before the scheduled public torture of Chögtrul Rinpoche, the senior *khenpo* of Darthang requested Chögtrul Rinpoche to depart immediately for the pure realms. He also requested that Chögtrul Rinpoche take his principal disciples with him. Two hours later, while reciting the *Arya's* Prayer for Excellent Conduct, Chögtrul Rinpoche reached the stanza which reads, "For however vast the space may be, all sentient beings, without exception, are as vast. The karma and delusions of sentient beings are equally as vast, as is the extent of this prayer." Without any indication of physical illness or pain, Chögtrul Rinpoche dissolved his mind directly into the sphere of truth. The next day, the *khenpo* and three other *tulkus* suddenly passed from this world.

The author received this information regarding the passing of Chögtrul Rinpoche from Rinpoche's personal attendant, Trochu Pedma Dorje. After Chögtrul Rinpoche passed away, the Chinese Communists threw his precious body into a mass grave. A Chinese man, present at the time, later told Tulku Lhumpo of Dharthang monastery where Chögtrul Rinpoche's remains could be found. In 1982, Tulku Lhumpo, along with several *tulkus* and monks, found the remains and the clothes that he was wearing still intact. After carefully removing his precious bones and relics, they returned them to Darthang monastery. There they built a beautiful gold and copper stupa, one story high, and placed within it the remains of this extraordinary guru. This sacred stupa is presently an object of refuge and pilgrimage for the faithful in Tibet. Chögtrul Rinpoche's incarnation was born in the holy land of the *Aryas*, India, in 1964, the year of the Fire Horse. He presently resides at the new Palyul Namdroling monastery and is under the guidance of the third Drubwang Pedma Norbu Rinpoche.

Gojo Rago Chögtrul Rinpoche

Gojo Rago Chögtrul Rinpoche, Thubten Shedrub Gyatso, was the principal disciple of the third Karma Kuchen Rinpoche, Dongag Chökyi Nyima. He was born in 1889, the fifteenth *rabjung* year of the Earth Rabbit. From Chökyi Nyima, he received full ordination, mind ripening teachings on the common preliminary practices and extraordinary Great Perfection practices of Buddha in the Palm of the Hand, the main empowerments of the *Rinchen Ter Dzöd* and the entire *kama* and *terma* transmissions of the Palyul tradition. From the Buddha Vajradhara Azam Drugpa Drodul Lingpa, he received the mind ripening teachings of the *Longchen Nyingthig* and the Secret Treasury Cycle. From Orgyen Rinchen Lingpa, he received the revelation of *Avalokiteshvara's* mind accomplishment and others. From Mugsang Khenpo Sheizang, Gojo Rago Chögtrul received the *Bodhicharya Avatara*, *Dom Sum Nam-nge* (Three Vows), *Abidharma Kosha*, *Jamcho Kör* (*Maitreya's* Works) and others. He later became known as a great scholar. Khentsey Chökyi Lodrö gave him the *Dam Ngag Dzöd* (Treasury of Essential Instructions) and Mugsang Chötrul Lodrö gave the transmission of the precious *Kagyur*. Gojo Ragon Chögtrul studied grammar and poetry from Khewang Karma Tsepal. In brief, he received all the major transmissions of the Nyingmapa lineage without exception. Afterwards, he took up residence at Sogra retreat and gave many empowerments and transmissions, as well as opening a new scholastic college. As an ascetic yogi, he truly lived a life free from contrived needs, which was at this time, rare to find. Any offering he received was immediately offered to erect the supports of enlightened body, speech and mind. Gojo Rago Chögtrul was a true servant of the doctrine, fulfilling the needs of whoever met him. From the depth of his heart, he worked to benefit the Palyul tradition in whatever way possible, be it directly or indirectly. Throughout the land of Tibet, the fame of his purity in *vinaya* discipline and scholarship spread. At the completion of his life's activities, his collected works amounted to four great volumes. During the Cultural Revolution, in 1972, the year of the Water Rat on the eighth day of the fifth month, at age ninety-three, he passed from this world.

The First Dzongnang Rinpoche

The first Dzongnang Jei Bon, Lama Kunzang Gyurmed, was born in the ancestral heritage of Kunzang Sherab, in the family of Droshin Phugtog of Palyul. As a child, he entered the door of the doctrine and was ordained as a novice monk by the third Karma Kuchen Rinpoche, Do-ngag Chökyi Nyima. Under the care of Dzongnang Lama Tashi, he received and practiced all of the empowerments, transmissions and commentaries of the Palyul tradition. When Do-ngag Chökyi Nyima passed away, he took over the administration of the Palyul monastery. While handling the administration of the mother monastery, the second Drubwang Pedma Norbu often spoke of his great kindness, for it was due to Kunzang Gyurmed's assistance that Pedma Norbu, as throne holder, was free to receive and bestow all the necessary empowerments, transmissions and teachings. Kunzang Gyurmed's pure motivation and efforts for the benefit of the doctrine were far reaching. At Palyul and Mugsang monasteries he erected new prayer wheels. He was extremely learned in all aspects of ritual practice such as chanting and lama dancing, and for many years he was the master instructor of the root dance of the illusory manifestations. In 1910, the year of the Iron Dog, when the Chinese King Ambar took spiritual and secular control of Do-Med, Kunzang Gyurmed was active in acquiring funds for the monasteries to continue the tenth day vase accomplishment offering ceremonies. With great respect and faith for the second Drubwang Pedma Norbu, he served his every need. He always oversaw the discipline of the monastery's regular schedule and kept things going during the most difficult times.

When the Tibetan government overthrew the Chinese occupation of Do Med, peace and happiness was once again restored. During this period of time, Kunzang Gyurmed acquired more farm land for the monastery's support. He obtained and cared for the new reincarnation of the third Karma Kuchen Rinpoche, Do-ngag Chökyi Nyima, oversaw his enthronement, tutoring and transmissions which were received at the Palyul monastery. He purchased many new offering materials for the monastery, including ten sets of ornamented gold and silver vases and five hundred new offering bowls. When his activity for the doctrine was complete, Kunzang Gyurmed passed away. The second Drubwang Pedma Norbu attended to Kunzang Gyurmed at the time of his passing and performed the traditional offering ceremonies.

His incarnation, the second Dzongnang Rinpoche Jampal Lodrö, was born in the Nyinmo family heritage of his predecessor's attendant and was clearly recognized by the second Drubwang Pedma Norbu Rinpoche. As a child, his character was naturally good. His teachers were his uncle, Lama Jamyang and Khenpo Lodrö. From the fourth Karma Kuchen Rinpoche, he received the *Nam Chö*, Ratna Lingpa's *termas, Kagyed Sang Dzog* (Complete Secret Eight *Herukas*), *Gongdu* (Condensed Enlightened Mind) and many other empowerments. From Chögtrul Rinpoche he received the *Rinchen Ter Dzöd*, from Khenpo Legshed Jordan, the *Dam Ngag Dzöd* (Treasury of Essential Pith Instructions) and from Khenpo Nuden Khentse Lodrö, his newly written commentary on the *sutras*. From Khenpo Asher of Kathog, Khenpo Gangshar of Shechen and Khenpos Lodrö and Gondrub of Palyul, Jampal Lodrö received teachings on many major scriptures.

The author of this book taught Jampal Lodrö writing, grammar, literature, poetry, astrology, mandala ritual practice and chanting. His comprehension of all subjects was supreme. For three consecutive years, he stayed at Darthang monastery and received, from Chögtrul Rinpoche, the extensive *Nam Chö* Great Perfection empowerments, transmissions and commentaries. From Lama Pedma Jigmed, he received the precious *Kagyur* transmission and many of Khenpo Ngaga's minor works. Later, Jampal Lodrö helped to administer Darthang Monastery and was a major benefactor for the annual lama dances held at the end of the old year. Although Jampal Lodro had purchased large amounts of cloth to make a huge tent for the monastery, when the Chinese occupation occurred, he was unable to complete this project. Realizing that extreme difficulties and hardships were imminent, Jampal Lodrö traveled to India, the land of the Aryas, passing by way of Gojo.

Arriving in India, Jampal Lodrö built Ngedön Gatsel Ling monastery (Pleasure Garden of Ultimate Truth) and Palyul Chökhor Ling monasteries in northern India. Following this he established the International Buddhist Education Institute in India and Thekchog Odsal Palyul Chöling Dharma Center in Kathmandu, Nepal. In recent years Dzongnang Rinpoche Jampal Lodrö has established the Taiwan Nyingmapa Palyul Dharma Center in Taipei, Taiwan, Republic of China. Like great waves, his activities are of unfailing benefit for the doctrine and living beings. With a pure mind of faith and fervent regard, the heartfelt prayer is offered that the second Dzongnang Rinpoche, Jampal Lodrö, may place his lotus feet in this world for one hundred aeons and that the author may once again be able to see his stainlessly compassionate and joyous face.

Top: The mother Palyul monastery before the Cultural Revolution, Kham, Tibet. Above: Present day Palyul monastery. Left: Three caves used by early masters of the Palyul lineage, including Kyerei Chökyong Wangpo.

*Right: The second Palyul
Chogtrul Rinpoche. Below:
Tulku Thupzang, reincarna-
tion of Thubten Palzang, do-
ing lama dancing at the
Palyul monastery, Tibet.*

Above: Namdroling Palyul monastery, Bylakuppe, South India. Left: The Second Dzongnang Rinpoche, Jampal Lodro, with photographs of Ngedon Gatsel Ling (left) and Palyul Chökhur Ling.

Khenpo Namdrol and the Fifth Karma Kuchen Rinpoche at Namdroling monastery, South India.

Jampal Lodrö Rinpoche, Tulku Ahkön Norbu Lhamo, Pedma Norbu Rinpoche, and Gyatrul Rinpoche together in Kathmandu, Nepal, May 1987.

Jampal Dorje

Jampal Dorje, the senior *khenpo* of Palyul, was born in the ancestral heritage of Kunzang Sherab into the Dongu family in the Ahchog area of Palyul. As a youth he took ordination from the third Karma Kuchen Rinpoche, Do-ngag Chökyi Nyima, and received his first teachings on the *Bodhicharya Avatara* from Mugsang Khenpo Lerab Dorje. From the Dzogchen Khenpos, Shenga Rinpoche, Sod Chö and so forth, he received teachings on many of the major volumes of *sutra* and *tantra* and practiced them well. In particular, Jampal Dorje stayed in the presence of the omniscient Lama Mipham Rinpoche for a long time, receiving many teachings directly from him. When the second Drubwang Pedma Norbu opened the scholastic college, Chökhor Norbu Ling, the first *khenpo* was Khenpo Ngaga Rinpoche. The main teachers were Pedma Norbu himself, Khenpo Rigzin Odzer of Dzogchen, Tro Kyab Geshe and Khenpo Jampal Dorje. Khenpo Jampal Dorje continued to teach at the scholastic college for an extended period of time and held the position of principal and *yarney khenpo* until he passed away. Eventually, the students themselves and became qualified *khenpos*, able to teach in the college. Jampal Dorje offered each of the fifty students in the college new robes and special ceremonial hats (from the *Gongdu Terma*). He was well known for the immensity of the offerings he always made during the final grand offering ceremony, occurring at the conclusion of each *yarney*. Because Jampal Dorje was so skillful in dealing with secular affairs, he rendered great assistance to the monastery during the turmoil of the Chinese takeover, temporarily safeguarding the monastery and lamas from harm or destruction. He gave regular teachings and transmissions for the *Nyingma Gyud Bum* to the third Karma Kuchen Rinpoche.

Learned in all the major volumes of *sutra* and *tantra*, Jampal Dorje especially ascertained the naked truth of the Non-dual Great Seal *Mahamudra*-Great Perfection *Ati Yoga* teachings. Due to his realization, he became the principal teacher for the preliminary and foundational practices of clear light *togyal*, darkness practice and all the advanced secret practices performed in the Palyul retreat center. Having fully completed his life's activities of benefiting this great Doctrine of Accomplishment, Khenpo Jampal Dorje passed from this world.

Dawa Odzer

The younger brother of the fourth Karma Kuchen Rinpoche was Dawa Odzer, who was born in 1916, the fifteenth *rabjung* year of the Fire Dragon. He was the reincarnation of Chagra Tulku of Chamdo and was recognized by the Tsongkor Mahasiddha Lama Dorje Chang. Right from childhood, Dawa Odzer possessed inherent, fully endowed wisdom qualities and strong enthusiastic perseverance in studies. From Azom Gyalsei Rinpoche, he received extensive secret oral transmission instructions and perfected all pure qualities and signs on the path. Afterwards, he took charge of the administration of the Palyul branch monastery of Ragchab. While running the monastery, he also completed many root recitations and accomplishment practices. From Khenpo Ngaga, Dawa Odzer received full ordination and became an honorable upholder of discipline. Later, when the Communist Chinese began occupying Tibet, he was given a position of authority in the Chinese administration.

17 Conclusion

Each of the great throne and lineage holders of the Palyul tradition became well known as great scholars of *sutra, tantra* and the outer and inner sciences. The Nyingma tradition is upheld as and destined to be the tradition of scriptural realization and meditative accomplishment. The view and meditation of the Great Perfection *Ati Yoga* is considered to be the most exalted and the most difficult to meet. Those with the karmic connection to practice this tradition are fortunate holders of a most precious jewel.

The successive throne holders and monks of the mother and branch Palyul monasteries practice the *vinaya* code of ethics as the foundational discipline. The emphasis on the practice of acceptance and rejection has produced a personal quality that has been a distinguishing characteristic of the practitioners of this tradition. Upon this foundation, the second root practice, the mind training of the great vehicle of *Mahayana* called the *bodhicitta* is placed. The aspirant trains to develop both aspirational and practical *bodhicitta* for the purpose of benefiting all sentient beings.

The tradition of practice that these highly disciplined monks strictly enforced has caused the Palyul lineage to become known as the tradition of accomplishment. The first practice in this accomplishment tradition is the thirty day preliminary practice retreat. This is followed by the forty-four day *tummo tsa-lung* practice; the 400,000 repetitions of the preliminary practices; the forty-day *togyal* transmission; the forty-day inner clear light *togyal* practice; the thirty-day darkness practice; the training in sound; the dream state; and the pure realms. Each of these practices are undergone according to the practitioner's level of understanding and realization. At the conclusion of each level, examinations are given which must be passed before moving onward to the next level. When all the requirements are fulfilled, the practitioner is then qualified to enter the three year retreat, although this is not mandatory.

During the three year retreat, the recitations of the Three Roots *(Lama, Yidam, Khandro)* are performed and accomplished, followed by the practice of *trekchöd (Ati Yoga).* The successful completion of the three year retreat is marked by achieving all the signs of true accomplishment, after which the practitioner receives enthronement and the title of *Vajra Acharya* (Tantric Master), which allows for the wearing of the traditional *Vajra Acharya* hat. Only at this time is the practitioner fully authorized as a qualified spiritual teacher (lama) with the potential to give empowerments, transmissions, teachings, special ceremonies and practices for the purpose of benefiting sentient beings. This excellent establishment of pure traditional conduct and practice in the Palyul tradition is originally due to the strength and kindness of the great Vidyadhara Kunzang Sherab, whose inconceivable compassion, activities and prayers continue to the present day.

The chariot of excellent merit pulls the sun
Of the tradition of the Khenpo, Lopon and King (Nyingmapa),
Ever illuminating this garden of the great Secret Doctrine.
The supreme, pristine petals of scriptural
And practical realization beautify this world.

When the wondrous sails of pure intention are elevated
The ship of the Secret Doctrine's deep meaning sails.
This history reveals the way
Of finding the jewel of profound purpose.
If there is the good fortune
Of knowing how to carefully investigate,
Then this book is a true cause for great joy.

In Palyul the excellent land of great mahasiddhas,
A Garland of Immortal Wish-Fulfilling Trees is born.
Blossoming from the tip of the branches
Of the nine characteristics of scholarship and accomplishment
Are the beautiful garlands of white lotus flowers
Of the Supreme Vehicle.

The life stories of the great lamas are vast like space
And my mind is like a bee searching for the limits of space.
Even though (I have) made many mistakes
Due to personal limitations,
I have written this book with the intention to fulfill the wishes
Of those great beings who guide and liberate others.

The pure water of the excellent speech of the earlier scholars
Has poured into (my) vessel of pure intention.
With the tip of the finger of the three levels of faith,
I offer this book,
Written free from the stain of pretext or untrue explanations.

If, because of the confusion of misunderstanding
And incorrect comprehension,
The pure mirror of their lives has been
Temporarily soiled by these accounts,
I implore those learned ones to kindly cleanse it
So the beautiful design of the meaning of their lives
Will be luminously clear.

May all the merit accumulated through the efforts of this work,
And the flow of all virtue accumulated in the three times,
Unite with the great ocean of Full Awakening.
May the doctrine of the Nyingmapa never decrease,
Remaining firm until the end of cyclic existence.

In Palyul monastery, the perfectly pure doctrine
Is propagated, (like the) realm of Kachöd,
Where all the manifestations of Buddha arise.
Whosoever has a karmic connection,
Including the sangha, is guided on the path to liberation.
May this great dharma center remain forever in this world.

Mt. Meru, composed of the molecules of the Buddha's three secrets,
Is a great jewel of powerful accomplishment,
Surrounded by an unending chain of golden mountains
Of doctrine upholders.
May the Buddha's doctrine continue to adorn this realm
And remain forever more.

Based on the foundation of pure morality,
The excellent assembly of the Arya Sangha is born.
From the ever-increasing goodness of the lotus garden sangha,
The stamen tips of the pure qualities of the three trainings arise
Issuing the abundant and rich sweet nectar
Of the nine great characteristics of scholarship.

When the elephant is intoxicated by the poison
Of incorrect prayers,
He wields the weapon of negative, barbaric customs in his trunk.
At this time, when he destroys the countries
Of the Buddha's doctrine,
May the clawed snow lion of the Three Jewels
Possess the potency to conquer!

May all beings who are trapped by the darkness
Of their own deluded karma,
See the moonlight of the spiritual teacher
And the friendly path of the ten virtues.
Liberated from falling over the cliff
Of their (own) negative perceptions,
May they arrive at the dwelling place
Of the All-Knowing Ones.

May I, in all my lifetimes, be protected
By the illuminating great wisdom light of compassion
Of the primordial sun,
And by actualizing the clear light
Pure-awareness-emptiness nature of mind,
May I possess the potential to serve the Buddha's Doctrine.[1]

The powerful sun of the Buddha
Is the perfected path of acceptance and rejection.
The Dharma treasure of nectar is the peaceful,
Cooling moon of non-attachment.
The Sangha is the garland of stars
And constellations of perceptive and actual awareness.

This book of the history of the successive throne holders of the
Palyul monastery and of the origin of the Palyul tradition was re-

quested by the third Drubwang Pedma Norbu Rinpoche and his attendant Gelong Tsedrug. The request came to the author, in Tibet, from the far away seat of Thekchog Namdrol Shedrub Dargye Ling monastery, in South India. Also in Tibet, Thubten Palzang Rinpoche and many concerned practitioners made persistent requests to the author to write this treatise. Drawing from the table of contents of the great Nyingma *Kama*, the works of Rago Chögtrul Rinpoche, and from the treasure of my own life's experience, I, Jampal Zangpo, a monk from Mugsang, began to write this book in my eighty-second year. By the grace of the precious lineage-holding gurus, in 1982, the year of the Water Dog, on the tenth day of the fifth month (the sacred birthday of Padmasambhava), this book was completed. The place where the book was composed is called Karma Lhateng, a sacred, isolated place, surrounded by juniper trees, where great realized masters, such as Kathog Ado Gyaltsen, Horpo Khechog Shakya Gyaltsen and others achieved realizations. May the virtue of this work spread the precious Nyingmapa Doctrine of the three inner *tantras* to all directions and times to increase and remain in this world forever!

*   *   *

In 1986, the year of the Fire Tiger, at the request of the third Drubwang Pedma Norbu Rinpoche, the first draft of the English translation was prepared at Palyul Thekchog Namdrol Shedrub Dargye Ling. The translators Sangye Khandro and Ngawang Paljor based the translation on commentaries and explanations given by the third Pedma Norbu Rinpoche and Khenpo Namdrol. The final copy of the translation was completed the same year at Tashi Chöling, the retreat center for Yeshe Nyingpo, south of Ashland, Oregon, United States of America.

Appendix 1: Palyul Branch Monasteries

The mother Palyul monastery, like a victory banner of the Buddha's doctrine, is maintained through the process of mental examination and realization. Placed upon the peak of existence by the *Chakravartin's* golden hand of knowledge and miraculous action, the branch Palyul Monasteries uphold, increase and spread this pure spiritual tradition.

The following is a list of the major and minor branch Palyul monasteries:

1. *Mugsang Sangngag Chöling* monastery was the principal seat of Kunzang Sherab's guru, Serlo Tönpa Gyaltsan, and his brother Nyima Gyaltsan, as well as one of Kunzang Sherab's direct disciples, Dorje Kunzang Gyatso.

2. *Ba Khyim* monastery was the seat of Kunzang Sherab's guru, Palmo Sherab Gyatso, and also the principal seat of the Dharma Lord Kathogpa Dampa Desheg Rinpoche. On the top level of this monastery, the illusory manifestation mandala of deities was drawn on a flat board. When the drawing wore away with time, actual flowers, in the pattern of the mandala spontaneously grew from the board. The flowers vividly displayed the mandala's entrances, partitions, and all important details. Since that time, a clear cut circumambulation path has been worn around the mandala's perimeter. Since this path could not possibly have been the work of human beings, it was made by the constant circumambulation of formless gods and spirits. Labtön Namkha Rinchen and Ado Konchog Gyaltsen stayed in *Ba Khyim* monastery for an extended period of time. Many lamas with perfected meditative realization came to this place. Among them were Lama Sherab Gyatso, Yontan Gyatso, Tashi Gyatso and others. *Ba Khyim* monastery also became known as a pure source of the *Maha, Anu* and *Ati Yogas*. At this monastery, all one hundred deities of the Life and Liberation of

Padmasambhava were carved in wood block. Mipham Rinpoche said that this particular wood block was an authentic, original reference for the study of Padmaambhava's life and activities.

3. *Gajei Kham-ü* monastery was one of the precious centers of the Nyingmapa tradition and initially, the seat of Trulshig Khenpo Sola Wangtrag Gyatso and Chökyong Gyatso. Chökyong Gyatso, an emanation of Vajrapani, was the first guru of Kunzang Sherab and a student of Gyatong Tönpa Senge. Other great lamas who came to this monastery include Gala Lhundrub Gyatso, Tashi Gyatso, Gaje Drasar Lama Sangngag Tendzin (the teacher from whom Jamgon Kongtrul Rinpoche many times received teachings from the old and new traditions). Gaje Sherab Tendar, who also stayed at the Mindroling monastery, Chögtrul Dorje Namgyal, Chögtrul Asang Norbu and many other important lineage holders of the Nyingmapa doctrine.

The following monasteries, which were regional branch monasteries, were built by the Vidyadhara Kunzang Sherab's four principal disciples from Hor.

4. *Lhatsey* monastery was the seat of Serpa Yeshe Senge, one of Kunzang Sherab's four great disciples from Hor. This monastery housed five hundred monks.

5. *Tsangda* monastery was the seat of Tsangda Dorje, one of Kunzang Sherab's four great disciples from Hor, housing four hundred monks.

6. *Jang-gang* monastery was the seat of Jang-gang Ahphel, one of the four great disciples from Hor, housing four hundred monks.

7. *Shug-gang* monastery was the seat of Lama Shug-gang Bading, one of the four great disciples of Kunzang Sherab, housing three hundred monks.

8. *Tsakho Odsal* monastery was the seat of Tsakho Tsondru Gyatso.

9. *Golog Darthang* monastery, also known as Do Ngag Shedrub Ling, was the main Palyul branch monastery, housing one thousand monks.

The last five monasteries listed were regional branch monasteries, meaning monks from each respective region would attend the local regional monastery for training, rather than going to the mother Palyul monastery.

The following monasteries gradually arose from the main

regional branch monasteries:
10. *Gya Kha Sadu Padma Od Ling;* 500 monks
11. *Kho Si Tsondru;* 300 monks
12. *Tro Chu Sa Töd*
13. *Lubar*
14. *Namka Teng*
15. *Sogmo Garchog*
16. *Dampa Sertog*
17. *Tob Chu*
18. The three monasteries of *Gojo, Töd* and *Med*, including *Zigag Norbu Ling* monastery.
19. Several minor monasteries in Chötsei.

The following monasteries are located in the region of Trokyab:
20. *Saog*
21. *Drubza*
22. *Kundza*
23. *Yidung*
24. *Tami*
25. *Tarku*
26. *Lan-o*
27. *Gowo*
28. *Kyabi*
29. *Shadam* and many minor branch monasteries.
30. *Tsamrin*
31. *Darthang* (mentioned earlier)
32. In lower Golog, *Rongön Chöling*
33. *Dzi Töd dram Gang*
34. *Dzi Rong*
35. *Dhida Dechen*
36. *Benchen*
37. *Babshi*
38. *Ü-tsa*
39. *Bernag*
40. *Dong Dzong*

The following monasteries are located in the region of Serkhog:
41. *Dribza*
42. *Gurdong*
43. *Gya-ü Thog*
44. *Sangdra*

45. *Rinang*
46. *Tengye*
47. *Ü-tsa*
48. *Trig-nang*
49. *Wag Tong*
50. *Chan-nga*
51. *Lulhe*
52. *Chungyu*
53. *Nagring*
54. *Nubzo*
55. *Gyashug*
56. *Nyi Shar*
57. *Sing Sing Dungkar Gyatong* monastery
58. *Chi-ngun* monastery and many other minor monasteries.

The following monasteries are located in the region of Ni Khog:
59. *Tsanchen*
60. *Lagor*
61. *Singtsang*
62. *Do med Tashi Chöling;* three hundred monks
63. *Wonpo.*

The following monasteries are located in the region of Ni Khog:
64. *Tsanchan;* three hundred monks
65. *Shugney* Retreat Center
66. *Gochen*
67. *Chog Ked*
68. *Arkyab Kharleb*
69. *Chög Tsang Tag Lung;* one thousand monks
70. *Nyilung Sera;* one thousand monks
71. *Bumshug;* three-hundred-fifty monks.

The following monasteries are located in the region of Litsang:
72. *Litöd Dhomang;* five hundred monks
73. *Limad Ahsug*
74. *Tsangmed Senge;* five hundred monks
75. *Raho;* five hundred monks
76. *Sago*
77. *Kuntsar.*

The following monastery is in the region of Mugnyag:
78. *Shigog Mugnyag.*

The following monastery is in the region of Dza Khog:

79. *Dza Khog Rakor.*
When the First Karma Kuchen Rinpoche, Karma Tashi came back from China, he built many large and small monasteries in the Dza Khog area, including Dardo Yigchung monastery.

80. *Ragkyab Samtan* monastery was the seat of the great Mani Rinchen, *mahasiddhi* of the rainbow body. Labtön Namkha Rinchen received spiritual authorization directly from *Mahakala* in this monastery. He made a statue of *Mahakala* which the primordial wisdom being entered into and blessed; the statue is kept in the monastery's protector temple. The monastery also has a retreat center. The yogi, Pedma Yeshe (Kunzang Sherab's younger brother) was appointed to be in charge of this retreat center. Later, Gadthog Lama took charge of the monastery and developed a very close relationship with the First Karma Kuchen Rinpoche, Karma Tashi. As a result, the monastery grew much larger and eventually housed five hundred monks.

81. *Shenchen Namdrab,* located in the sacred place of Dzam Thog
82. *Chagra Ewam,* the seat of Jatsa Lama
83. *Wön Töd Lhadrang*
84. *Polo Gurei Namgyal*
85. *Barong Drungyig*
86. *Palbar Lhathang*
87. *Tsamdo Ogthang*
88. *Nyagshi Rigo*
89. *Shugag*
90. *Manshei Rigo*
91. *Pedma Odsal Sangngag Chöling*
92. *Jesub*
93. *Kharchu*
94. *Pomed Gaden*
95. *Gonkyid Dechen*
96. *Achög Yagdra*
97. *Rushe Samdrub*
98. *Othang*
99. *Dragmar*
100. *Ahtri*
101. *Lugar*
102. *Yudrug*
103. *Mo Kathog*

104. *Dongdra Dzongo*
105. *Yarla Dawa*
106. *Kutsei Gei*
107. *Singte*
108. *Gongo*
109. *Nyashi Wadong*
110. *Lhobo Rigo*
111. *Banag,* founded by the Second Drubwang Pedma Norbu Rinpoche
112. *Samdrub* and many minor monasteries, all founded by the Second Drubwang Pedma Norbu Rinpoche.

The following monasteries are located in the region of Gojo:
113. *Do Tod Khaleg Chögar*
114. *Ngulra*
115. *Raggo*
116. *Rago Sogra* Retreat Center
117. *Tsaru*
118. *Gyara*
119. *Ritrod Yang*
120. *Lungphug*
121. *Kyathang*
122. *Tharra*
123. *Kyilphug*
124. *Chogyal*
125. *Lhuphug*
126. *Gangpo*

The second Chögtrul Rinpoche said, "If one were to count the number of monks in the Palyul branch monasteries, from the Chinese border to Palyul, the total would exceed twenty thousand. Many of the major and minor monasteries are listed; however, there were many other branch monasteries located in the Domed area of Kham.

Appendix 2: Source of the Nyingma Tradition

The *Gyud Lama Tantra* states, "Just as the powerful gods see the foundational earth as pure lapis lazuli, upon which the reflection of form appears, similarly, sentient beings perceive the pure foundational earth upon which the reflection of the form of the Buddha appears."

As this quote indicates, the triple *kaya* pure realms of the Buddhas arise in dependence upon the strength of the positive merit of sentient beings. For instance, although the moon mandala in space is omnipresent, it is only directly perceived on earth through the power of a vessel containing water to purely reflect it there. If there is no water-containing vessel on the earth, there will be no support for the form of the moon to reflect. Some extremely deluded individuals are temporarily prevented from actualizing pure faith and pure perception, and even go so far as to harm and attempt to destroy conventional images of the Buddha. On the other hand, individuals of superior intelligence, such as Indrabhuti, having cleared away delusions without effort or difficulty, directly perceive the *Dharmakaya* Buddha in this world.

The loving kindness and strength of the Buddha's prayers is inconceivable and undiminishing. Within every pore on the body of the great Shakyamuni Namnang Gangchen Tso are inconceivable numbers of pure realms. Inside the begging bowl he holds in his two hands is an ocean of perfumed water and, in the center a magnificent flower, which has twenty-five sequentially arranged pure realms, thirteen of which are arranged at the level of his heart. These thirteen are known as Mijed Jigten, the name of our world system. Within Mijed Jigten are numberless *Dharmakaya*, *Sambhogakaya* and *Nirmanakaya* pure realms, appearing in dependence upon the aspirations and prayers of beings whose delusions still remain untamed. For such common beings with ordinary perception, the *Nirmanakaya* pure realm appears. In this fortunate aeon of ours, 1,002 *Nirmanakaya* Buddhas will appear to liberate beings. We are presently experiencing the time period of the fourth *Nirmanakaya* Buddha, Shakyamuni. As it states in the *Dulcha Wang gi Chi Do Sutra*, "On the path there are various vehicles such as those of renunciation, of bearing hardships and of transformation through skillful means." According to this tradition, the Nyingmapa, there are nine such vehicles on the path to realization, both common and extraordinary. The outer or common vehicles of renunciation practice are the vehicles of hearers, solitary realizers and *bodhisattvas*. The inner vehicles of bearing hardships on the path are the *Kriya, Upa, Charya* and *Yoga Tantras*. The secret vehicles of transformation through skillful means are the *Maha, Anu* and *Ati Yoga Tantras*. The views and practice found in the Nyingma tradition are rooted primarily within the latter three vehicles.

Maha Yoga is a Sanskrit title which means "the yoga of great action." This *Tantra* is comprised of the generation stage, corresponding to method. Within *Maha Yoga* are the two classes of *tantra* and accomplishment.

Anu Yoga means "the yoga which follows," primarily comprised of the completion stage, which corresponds to wisdom. This includes all the root *tantras* and explanatory *tantras*, such as *Dupa Do* and others.

Ati Yoga means "the extreme yoga," which indivisibly unites the generation and completion stages. It is divided into the mind class, basic expanse class and pith essential instruction class. These class divisions are elaborated upon in depth in the extensive Treatise on the Origin of Dharma.

The nine vehicles are distinguished by their difference in profundity and swiftness. This difference moves from the lower to higher vehicles. For instance, the hearers only philosophically adhere to the identity-less-ness of self. The solitary realizers take that one step further by ascertaining identity-less-ness of self and partial ascertainment of the identity-less-ness of appearances. Similarly, the secret mantra vehicles are more advanced than the vehicle of *bodhisattvas*. As the Buddha said, "Although the one truth is universal, the tantric vehicle is sublime with its various methods practiced by those of superior intelligence, without having to undergo many hardships."

In *tantra*, the view, meditation, conduct, result and ground of practice in *Upa Yoga* is more advanced than in *Kriya Yoga*. The *Yoga tantra* is similarly more advanced than *Upa Yoga*. These differences and pure qualities are elaborated upon in depth in the Omniscient Longchenpa's Seven Treasures and Treasury of Pure Qualities.

According to the later translation schools, known as Sarma, there are four tantric vehicles which are *Kriya, Upa, Yoga* and *Maha Anuttarayoga Tantras*. They correspond to the three secret vehicles of *Maha, Anu* and *Ati Yoga*. By looking into the *tantras* to discover these distinctions and through hearing and contemplation, conclusions may be derived through correct understanding.

The following is a general explanation of how the unsurpassed secret mantra vehicle came into this world: According to the uncommon explanation of the Nyingmapa tradition, in the great Buddha Realm of Akanishtha, the nature of the Buddha and the assembly is indivisibly one, free from sound, words or expression. The nature of this self-expression appears as the five uncommon *Sambhogakaya* pure realms and the common *Nirmanakaya* realms where sentient beings are tamed, according to destiny. Due to this, we have the three lineages of Mind-to-Mind Transmission, Symbolic Indication of Pure-Awareness Beings, and Oral Transmission for ordinary individuals. These three lineages have gradually led gods, *nagas*, humans and countless sentient beings to the result of bodhisattvahood, in the mode of the three protector-*bodhisattvas*, *Manjusri, Chenresig* and *Vajrapani*.

In particular, concerning the unsurpassed tantric vehicles, our own Buddha Shakyamuni prophesied that twenty-eight years after his *paranirvana*, the Five Exalted Sages would arise simultaneously from their respective *samadhis* to gather together and pray with intense yearning devotion. Due to that interdependent condition, a scripture of the *Maha Yoga* accomplishment class descended from the sky to the roof of King Dza's temple. Along with the enlightened activities of *Arya Nagarjuna*, the eight great *mahasiddhas* of India and many other sages of the time, the propagation of *tantra* was well underway in the world of human beings. According to prophecy, it also came to pass that the great Acharya Padmasambhava, through his great unceasing kindness, journeyed to Tibet, the land of snows, to bring these doctrines of *tantra* that were flourishing in India.

Following is a brief explanation of how the doctrine spread in Tibet: The *Jampal Tsa Gyud Tantra* states, "the dry lakes in the snow land of Tibet will transform into lush foliage and forests." This prophecy indicates that a transformation was to take place. Indeed, through the union of a monkey (the emanation of *Chenresig*) and a rock demoness (the emanation of *Jetsun Drolma*), the original lineage of human beings in Tibet was produced. After the passing of many years, all of Tibet came under the rule of King Nyatri. Twenty-eight dynasties later, during the reign of King Lhato Thonyentsen, an emanation of the *Bodhisattva* Kuntuzangpo, the prophecy from the *sutra Lhamo Drimamedpa Do* came to pass: "Twenty-five hundred years after I pass into *nirvana*, the dharma will spread in the land of red-faced people." Accordingly, upon the roof of the king's palace, Yumbu Lhakhang, the *Do Zama Tog* and other holy scriptures descended. This began the spread of the dharma in Tibet.

Five royal lines later, *Chenresig* took human form as the great dharma king, Songtsen Gampo. Through his miraculous powers he built the famed Jowo Cathedral and invited two images of Shakyamuni from China and India to be placed within. In addition the great emanation of *Manjusri*, Thonmi Sambhota, and other Indian pandits were invited to translate the sound of mantras and the outer and inner sciences from their original Sanskrit into a new Tibetan script. The original Tibetan syllables were composed and initially many *sutras* and *tantras* concerning *Chenresig* were translated. From that time, the precious dharma teachings were exemplified through the instigation of the ten virtuous deeds of gods and the sixteen pure dharmas of humans.

Five centuries later, the human emanation of *Manjusri*, the powerful king, Trisong Deutsen, appeared to take over the kingdom at the age of thirteen. Through his skillful miraculous actions, the dharma flourished. At his invitation, the Indian Bodhisattva Khenpo Shantarakshita came to Tibet to teach the eight branches, the ten virtues, eighteen elements and other discourses. Since the gods, spirits and negative entities in Tibet were so forbidding, the Khenpo suggested that the master tantric adept of India, Acharya Padmasambhava, be immediately invited to eradicate these interruptions.

According to prophecy, Padmasambhava was personally invited by the messenger Nanam Dorje Dudjom, and he entered Tibet through the direction of Mangyul Gungthang. Placing all the gods and demons of Tibet under his command, he met the dharma king and Khenpo, blessing and consecrating the land he tread upon. Sub-jugating all evil influences, he waved his vajra victoriously in space, blessing the entire land.

The unchanging, spontaneously accomplished temple, Samye of the three traditions, was erected, and Padmasambhava caused the creatures of negativity to work by night, as the humans worked by day. This famous Samye temple was comprised of Mt. Meru, the four continents, subcontinents, the sun, moon and the encircling iron fence. During the consecration ceremony, all the primordial wisdom deities actually appeared in the surrounding sky and dissolved into and consecrated the mandala. Everyone present witnessed the miracle and, after the consecration, the images spoke. The full account of this historical period of time is astonishing!

From this time onward, the *sutras* and *tantras* in their entirety were brought to Tibet and translated. The most skilled Tibetans were trained to be translators and 108 great *acharyas* were invited from India. The foundation for ordination was initiated by Khenpo Shantarakshita and the first seven men were ordained in Tibet.

In all of India, the qualities of Khenpo Shantarakshita and Pad-masambhava were unequalled. Because of their efforts, great scholars and 108 translators assembled to translate not only a few of the important scriptures, but virtually all of the difficult *sutras, tantras* and commentaries, without exception, into the Tibetan language. Not only translation, but teaching, hearing, meditation and accomplishment were experienced until realization of the inner meaning was actualized. The entire collection of *Mahayana Sutras* and *Tantras* was translated and actualized in a way greater than ex-isted even in India.

Since success on the path of secret mantra is dependent upon the qualifications of the vessel who practices it, Padmasambhava selected twenty-five disciples of superior karma, and passed on to them all the direct transmissions. They practiced accordingly and achieved *siddhis* (powers), such as flying in space like birds, swimm-ing underwater like fish, and passing through mountains and solid rock formation without impediment. All these miraculous achievements are recorded in detailed accounts of their individual life stories.

Although in India there were no distinctions between earlier and later translation schools, the time that all the *sutras* and *tantras* were translated in Tibet by the original translator Thonmi Sambhota, until the time of the great translator, Rinchen Zangpo, is known as the earlier translation period. All the *sutras* and *tantras* are known as the Dharma of the Nyingmapa (earlier translation school). All the practitioners became known as Nyingmapas.

The Nyingmapa school is further distinguished by three lineages. They are the long lineage of *kama*, the short lineage of *terma* and the profound lineage of pure vision. As time prevailed in the snow land of Tibet, the Nyingmapa was primarily propagated through six mother monasteries and traditions, which were Dorje Drag and Mindroling in the upper region, Sechen and Dzogchen in the central region and Kathog and Palyul in the lower region.

The following is a brief explanation of how the glorious and victorious Palyul Monastery and tradition began:

The clear light Great Perfection teacher, Garab Dorje, the emanation of Jetsun Drolma Gyaza Kongjo, the great translator, Berotsana, the magician Kyere Chökyong Wangpo and many other great *bodhisattvas*, all blessed the land which the Palyul monastery was built on. Located in the Bubor district of Do-Kham, the building of the Palyul Namgyal Changchub Chöling monastery was instigated by the strength of the ripening merit and power of the great dharma king of Dege, Lhachen Jampa Phuntsog. After completion, over five-hundred monks immediately gathered at the new monastic center. The great Vidyadhara Kunzang Sherab was invited to be the first supreme head of the monastery. In his past lifetimes, Kunzang Sherab had been Rigzin Garab Dorje, Lopon Shiri Singha, Jampal Shenyen, Indra Bodhi and many other well known *bodhisattvas*.

In the eleventh *rabjung* year of the Fire Rat, Kunzang Sherab awakened his true nature when he met his teachers, Terton Migyur Dorje, Karma Chagmed Rinpoche, Gaje Chökyong Gyatso, Drungpa Chönyid Gyatso, Gyawen Konchog Tashi, Serlo Tonpa Gyaltsen, Tertön Longsal Nyingpo and others, who introduced him to the three lineages in all their entirety. In particular, he received all the uncommon transmissions of the clear light Great Perfection, which includes every essential stage on the path to liberation in one lifetime. Without exception, Kunzang Sherab actualized all the transmissions through practice and he perceived his true nature. Perfecting the four visions of *togyal*, all signs of accomplishment on the path of Great Perfection were manifested as he recalled, in one instant, thousands of lifetimes. He then possessed full power of extra-perception and miraculous activity.

Kunzang Sherab was in his thirtieth year when he arrived at the Palyul monastery, having come at the invitation of the dharma king of Dege, Tertön Migyur Dorje and Serlo Tönpa Gyaltsen. After taking charge as the first throne holder he instigated the *Pratimoksha* training as the foundational discipline, upon which was applied the two traditions of *bodhisattva* training. The general dharma of *kama* and *terma* lineages was practiced and, more specifically, a focus upon the clear Great Perfection practices. These practices have been passed on and practiced according to disciples' abilities in an unbroken line since the time of Kunzang Sherab to the present. It is for this reason that the Palyul has become known as the "tradition of accomplishment."

From Kunzang Sherab the throne holders in succession have been: Pedma Lhundrub Gyatso, Drubwang Pedma Norbu, Karma Chöpal Zangpo, Tsungmed Karma Lhawang and Karma Döndam, Gyurmed Ngedon Tenzin, Pedma Do-ngag Tenzin, Do-ngag Chökyi Nyima, Rigzin Palchen Dupa, Karma Thekchog Nyingpo and Drubwang Jigmed Thubten Shedrub Chökyi Dra-yang Palzangpo (the third Drubwang Pedma Norbu). Although these great masters have their own lineage of disciples branching off, they remain as an unbroken golden chain from which miraculous activities swell like a springtime lake.

In particular, the eleventh throneholder and present teacher of our time is well known as an emanation of Vimalamitra. The third Drubwang Pedma Norbu has fully received all lineage transmissions, which he has actualized through practice until all pure qualities were manifest. He has built the Palyul monastery in South India, has rebuilt the Palyul monastery in Tibet, and has established the largest Nyingma scholastic college in the world today. On countless occasions, he has turned the precious Dharma Wheel, giving many major empowerments and transmissions, such as the Nyingma *Kama, Ka Gyed, Gongdu, Nam Chö, Ratna* and others. He continues to actively transmit the lineages and practices of the profound clear light Great Perfection.

It is with the deepest heartfelt gratitude, respect and faith that this book has been written, translated and published with the prayer that the pure Palyul tradition may continue to flourish and prevail throughout this world, that the life of the third Drubwang Pedma Norbu Rinpoche may be firm and unchanging, like a vajra, and that all beings may receive boundless benefit.

Notes

1   Six specific dharmas are the resultant state of the practice of the
    great-perfection *Ati yoga*. They are: exalted awareness of one's
    own foundational nature; awareness of one's own true face;ac-
    tualization of pure awareness; instantaneous liberation; aware-
    ness which is unoriginating from another source; the unmoving
    presence of pure awareness.
2   Chariots pulling the powerful sun refers to the Hindu
    mythological belief that the sun is drawn around the world by a
    chariot pulled by seven horses. In Buddhist poetry, the myth is
    employed to point out a deeper meaning.
3   The six great qualities of the supreme secret clear light refers to
    the six exalted qualities of the Nyingmapa school of the earlier
    translations. These six qualities are: the greatness of the original
    dharma benefactors; the greatness of the environment (Samye
    Migyur Lundrub temple); the greatness of the original
    translators (Berotsana, Kawapaltsig Choro-luyi Gyaltsen and
    others); the greatness of the original Pandits (Khenpo Shantarak-
    shita, Lopon Padmasambhava, Vimalamitra and others); the
    greatness of the mandala offerings, made to request the
    precious dharma wheel to turn in Tibet for the first
    time; the greatness of the meaning of the original dharma teach-
    ings and translations.
4   The nine characteristics of scholarship and accomplishment are:
    teaching; debate; composition; spiritual generosity; practice;
    dharma activities (building and erecting statues, stupas, temples,
    etc.); great knowledge of the *sutras* and *tantras;* moral
    discipline; superior conduct for the benefit of sentient
    beings.

5   Lake Manasarowara is one of a pair of large lakes lying at the foot of Mt. Kailash in Tibet. This lake is the source of the great rivers of Tibet and India.

6   The three worlds are the world of gods (above the earth), the world of humans (upon the earth) and the world of *nagas* (below the earth).

CHAPTER ONE:
THE SOURCE OF THE DHARMA LINEAGES

1   The eight categories in the *tantra* class of generation *Maha Yoga* are: the root *Tantra, Sangwai Nyingpo* (Secret Essence, revealing personal awareness of the nature of mind and primordial wisdom); the *Lhamo Gyutrul Drawa* (revealing the actual display); the *Gyutrul Gyedpa* (revealing the perfected mandala); the *Shi Chupa* (revealing perfected miraculous activity); the *Gyutrul Lhama* (revealing the principal empowerments); the *Gyed Chupa* (revealing the perfection of pure qualities); the *Jampal Gyutrul Drawa* revealing the all pervasiveness of the categories); the *Gyutrul Leilag* (revealing the supreme words of honor).

2   The four categories in the *tantra* class of transmission *Anu Yoga* are: the *Kundu Rigpai Do Naljor Drubpai Gyud* (in thirty-three chapters); *Sangye Thamched Kyi Gongpa Dupa Do* (in seventy-two chapters) *Yeshe Ngampa Lo-gyi Khorlo Thekpa Chenpo Do* (in seventeen chapters); *Dutrod Kushug Polpai Gyud Thekpa Chenpo Do* (in fourteen chapters).

3   The five earlier translations of the Great Perfection *Ati Yoga* mind class are: *Rigpai Kushug; Tsalchen Drugpa; Chungchen Dingwa; Dola Sershun; Minubpai Gyaltsen.* The thirteen later translations of the Great Perfection *Ati Yoga* mind class are: *Tsemo Jungyal; Namkhai Gyalpa; Dewa Trulkod; Dzogpa Chi Ching; Changchub Sem Rig; Dewa Rabjam; Sog Kyi Khorlo; Thigley Drugpa; Dzogpa Chi Chöd; Yidshin Norbu; Kundu Rigpa; Jetsun Dampa; Gompa Don.*

4   The seventeen categories of the Great Perfection *Ati Yoga* essential instruction class are: 1. *Senge Tsal Dzogchenpo Gyud* (in thirteen chapters); 2. *Yigi medpa Gyud Chenpo* (in six chapters); 3. *Nyima dang Dawa Khajorwa Chenpo Sangwai Gyud* (in four chapters); 4. *Rinpoche Pungpoi Yontan Chenpo Tongpai Gyud Kyi Gyalpo*

(in five chapters); 5. *Norbu Trakod Rangyi Don Thamched Salwar Chedpai Gyud* (in fourteen chapters); 6. *Pal Namkha Medpa Kudung Barwa Chenpo Gyud* (in six chapters); 7. *Ngotrod Rinpoche Tredpa Shing Kham Tenpai Gyud* (in three chapters); 8. *Rigpa Rangshar Chenpo Gyud* (in eighty-six chapters); 9. *Rigpa Rangdrol Chenpo Thamched Drolwai Gyud* (in six chapters); 10. *Rinpoche Jungwar Chedpa Dra Thalgyur Chenpoi Gyud* (in six chapters); 11. *Dorje Sempa Nying-Gyi Melong Gyi Gyud* (in eighteen chapters); 12. *Kuntuzangpo Thug Kyi Melong Gyi Gyud* (in seven chapters); 13. *Kuntuzangpo Long Drug pai Gyud* (in six chapters); 14. *Tashi Dzeden Chenpoi Gyud* (in seven chapters); 15. *Ku Thamched Kyi Nangwa Tönpa Wang Drogpa Rangjung Chenpoi Gyud* (in eight chapters); 16. *Mutig Rinpoche Trengwai Gyud* (in eight chapters); 17. *Ser gyi Metog Dzepa Rinpoche Dronma Barwai Gyud* (in four chapters).

5   The rainbow light body is the accomplishment of the intentional dissolution of the corporeal body into light molecules. At this period in time, many of Changchub Pal's disciples in the Kathog tradition achieved the rainbow light body at the time of death.

6   The golden lineages of the Kagyud tradition are the four major schools of Dagpo Kagyud, Tsalpa Kagyud, Karma Kagyud and Phagmo Drugpa Kagyud. The eight minor schools are the Drigung Kagyud, Taglung Kagyud, Trobu Kagyud, Lingje Kagyud, Yazang Kagyud, Nyipu Kagyud, Shugseb Kagyud and Martzang Kagyud.

7   Clear light *togyal,* inner *togyal,* darkness practice, dream practice, training in the nature of sound and pure realms practice are the successive stages of transmission and development that the practitioner must undergo. These are considered to be the most esoteric, secret teachings of the path of Buddhism and are the most profound practices in the Palyul tradition.

8   *Shiney* (peaceful abiding) is a meditative technique employed to achieve single-pointed concentration and the pacification of the mind. This practice is performed both with and without mental supports, depending on the level of the practitioner.

9   The three *kaya* accomplishment of Ratna Lingpa's *Thug Drub* (Mind Accomplishment) is performed annually at the Palyul monastery. During the first year, for one month, the *Nirmanakaya* Mind Accomplishment is performed. During the second year, for one month, the *Sambhogakaya* Mind Accomplishment

is performed and during the third year, for one month, the *Dharmakaya* Mind Accomplishment is performed.

CHAPTER TWO:
THE MOTHER PALYUL MONASTERY

1 Tsamdo is part of Palyul, located in the lower province of Dokham, and is one of the six regions called Bubor. This quote is included to further validate the location of the Palyul monastery in this sacred region.

2 "Four activities practice cave" refers to the place where Kyere Chökyong Wangpo practiced the generation of peaceful, extensive, powerful and wrathful activities, for the sake of developing methods which guide and liberate all sentient beings.

3 The *Sangdag* secret accomplishment cave is where Padmasambhava performed the secret accomplishment practice of *Vajrapani*, the keeper of the secret *Mantrayana*.

CHAPTER FIVE:
THE FIRST THRONE HOLDER

1 This secret prophecy of Sangye Lingpa's *Gongdu* revelation should be interpreted in the following way: Due to the kindness of King Trisong Deutsen, the monk Gendun Zangpo (Kunzang Sherab in his past life) became a holder of the secret *Gongdu* revelations. Gendun Zangpo's depth of understanding and realization was equal to the king and he greatly increased the *Gongdu* Doctrine. When he reincarnated, bearing the name *Prajna* (Sherab in Tibetan), he was destined to utilize this awareness of the profundity of *Gongdu* and in areas where there was no dharma and in areas that were extremely remote, he spread the *Gongdu* Doctrine, bringing great benefit to many beings. In his incarnation as Kunzang Sherab, he possessed the character of a hidden yogi (one who conceals their innermost powers from the general public) and his voice was clear, deep and melodious. He possessed boundless compassion that was equal only to space. Since the first dharma keeper of the *Gongdu* revelations was King Trisong Deutsen, Gendun Zangpo and his future incarnation,

Kunzang Sherab, became the next dharma regents, greatly increasing this Doctrine. When King Trisong Deutsen expelled Lotsawa Berotsana from the region of central Tibet, the *Gongdu* Doctrine declined as a karmic result. Gendun Zangpo made specific prayers to end this karma by taking it all upon himself and, through the force of these prayers, he was able to accomplish this, so that the *Gongdu* Doctrine was revived. "Dissolving into the king's heart" refers to the fact that as a dharma regent, he is of the same emanation and at the time of leaving his body, Gendun Zangpo's mind merged with the mind of the king and from the *Dharmakaya*, countless emanations continue to arise and manifest.

2   This secret prophecy refers to the fact that these lamas named Chagmed, Tsultrim and Zang (Kunzang) are dharma keepers of the *Nam Chö*. If they were marked by a mole on the nape of the neck, then the *Nam Chö* must be transmitted to them in order for the interdependent auspicious connection to be made for future transmissions and propagation. Kunzang Sherab is one of these three and he was marked by a mole on the nape of his neck.

3   This secret prophecy of Tertön Longsal Nyingpo's revelations refers to the dharma keepers. According to this prophecy, there will be six dharma keepers. Three will have the name Sherab (Wisdom). Since Kunzang Sherab's name contains the Sherab, he is recognized to be one of the dharma keepers. Tertön Longsal Nyingpo and Kunzang Sherab lived at the same time and the Tertön himself directly recognized Kunzang Sherab as a dharma keeper of his revelations.

4   *Rabjung* is the term used for the Tibetan system of counting, based on sixty year cycles, similar to the western century of one hundred years. When Lord Buddha Shakyamuni taught the *Kalachakra* (Wheel of Time) at Palden Drekar Pungpai Stupa, he prophesied that when Pedma Karpo's commentary of the *Kalachakra* was translated into the Tibetan language, it would mark the beginning of the first year of the first *rabjung* (sixty-year cycle). The first *rabjung* began in 1027 A.D., the year of the Female Fire Rabbit. The final year of the sixty year cycle is the year of the Fire Tiger. A *rabjung* is comprised of twelve animal signs, with five elements that rotate in successive order. The animals are the horse, sheep, monkey, bird, dog, pig, rat, ox,

tiger, rabbit, dragon and snake. The elements are fire, earth, iron, water and wood. Each animal appears with each one of five elements during the course of the sixty year cycle.

5   *Genyen,* lay-Buddhist ordination, is the first category of precepts, according to the *vinaya* of the Pratimoksha. To become a *genyen,* the aspirant must accept one, two, three, four or five vows. If all five vows are taken, the aspirant becomes a full-fledged *genyen.* The vows are to never kill, steal, commit adultery, speak dishonestly, or take intoxicants. These vows are taken for the duration of one's life. By maintaining the vows purely, great merit and virtue is accumulated.

6   A *jenang* (transference of power) authorizes the recipient to perform the corresponding practice. A *jenang* does not transmit the three extraordinary inner empowerments. The outer common empowerment, which corresponds to Buddha's body, is transmitted.

7   *Orgyen Vajradhara* is the *Dharmakaya-Sambhogakaya* aspect of Padmasambhava, which is only experienced by those of high realization.

8   The four spontaneously accomplished visions of *togyal* are: the direct perception of the *dharmata* (nature of truth); the increasing experience of that perception; the full magnitude of total pure awareness; and the exhaustion of all dharmas into the *dharmata* (nature of truth). These are the highest stages of realization in the Great Perfection *Ati Yoga,* the result of which is the rainbow body accomplishment.

9   The *Nyingma Gyud Bum* is the collection of all the transmissions of the Nyingma *Kama* lineage of the three inner yogas, *Maha, Anu,* and *Ati.* The *Nyingma Gyud Bum* was compiled by the great Tertön Ratna Lingpa.

10   The three wheels of miraculous activities are: the development of the wisdom of hearing and contemplation; the abandonment of obscurations and continual perseverance in meditation; and activities performed solely for the benefit of the doctrine and sentient beings.

11   *Gelong* or full ordination as a monk is the third and final category of vows taken in the *Pratimoksha* system. The second category is called *getsul* or novice ordination at which time one must receive vows from a *khenpo* (qualified scholar) and *lopon* (qualified teacher); then one becomes a renunciate. As

a *getsul*, the initial five vows of a *genyen* (lay-Buddhist) are taken; however, instead of abstinence from adultery, the vow of celibacy is embraced. The *getsul* also abandons alcohol, dancing, singing, the playing of musical instruments (these three are counted as one vow); wearing perfume, ornaments, make-up, keeping of gold, silver or personal savings (with the intention to use the money for something other than offerings to the Three Jewels), partaking of food after the mid-day meal and sitting upon or sleeping on an expensive, ornate bed that is higher than one cubit's length. In order to become a *gelong*, at least five other *gelongs* must be present to bestow the vows. All of these vows of the first two categories are taken, along with *gelong* vows, which total two hundred fifty-three. In the case of a female, the vows total three hundred sixty-four. The vows are taken for the duration of one's lifetime, bringing profound temporary and ultimate benefits. Temporarily,one will be reborn in higher states of rebirth and ultimately *Arhatship* will be achieved. If the vows are taken with that *Mahayana* motivation of *bodhicitta*, the result is the ultimate realization of perfect Buddhahood.

12   One hundred different objects of oblation refers to the strong tradition of generosity practiced in the *Vajrayana*. In the past, when the emperor of China took refuge with Drogon Chögyal Phagpa and while receiving empowerments and transmissions, the emperor offered his guru, Drogon Chögyal Phagpa, the entire land of Tibet. It is customary to offer the finest materials to one's initiating guru to express one's gratitude for the priceless gift of the dharma. Because of this, it later became customary to offer one hundred different excellent material items to emphasize this gratitude.

13   Twenty-four hour fasting and vow observance is a ceremony initially taken in the presence of a qualified lama. Thereafter, in the absence of a lama, one may take the vows in the presence of the Three Jewels of Refuge. The vows taken for a period of twenty-four hours, are the ten vows of a *getsul* (novice). This practice produces the causes which result in the ultimate realization of Buddhahood and the temporary achievement of higher rebirth as a human or god.

14   The supremely awakened mind is also called *bodhicitta*. In general, *bodhicitta* is the uncontrived sincere wish to achieve lib-

eration from cyclic existence for the sake of benefitting and lib-erating all parent sentient beings. When the commitment is made to lead one's life based on this motivation, *bodhicitta* vows are taken. These vows must be received formally from a qualified teacher. There are two lineages of *bodhicitta* vows, originating with Nagarjuna and Asanga. The *Longchen Nyingthig* tradition practices the lineage of Nagarjuna, which is said to be the most direct. The omniscient Longchenpa had a vision of Nagarjuna and received the vows and lineage directly at that time. The Mindroling tradition of Terdag Lingpa practices the most direct lineage of Asanga. Mindroling Terchen had a vision of Asanga and received, at that time, the vows and line-age directly. The Palyul tradition holds and practices both lineages.

15   The accumulation of 400,000 repetitions refers to the prac-tice of the uncommon Preliminaries. Here, the aspirant must perform 100,000 prostrations while reciting the verses of refuge and *bodhicitta* simultaneously. This is count-ed as 100,000. Similarly, 100,000 repetitions of the mandala offering, the one hundred syllable mantra of *Vajrasattva* and the mantra of Padmasambhava are repeated. In the end, 400,000 repetitions are accumulated to complete the required number.

16   The traditional wet cloth examination is always given at the conclusion of the *Nam Chö tummo* retreat. Ideally, this retreat is carried out during the coldest winter months. During this practice, the practitioner learns to give rise to the inherent pri-mordial wisdom fire that is self-igniting. The channels are un-knotted and re-opened so that the pure winds and essential fluids can once again flow freely and can be controlled and directed into the central energy channel. In the examination, each practitioner is given a dripping wet cloth to drape around his or her bare body. Then, in a matter of minutes, the cloth must be dried by giving rise to the inner *tummo* heat.

17   *Lhagtong,* or extra-perception in this context, is the practice and experience of the Non-dual Great Seal *Mahamudra*-Great Perfection *Ati Yoga.* The practitioner is introduced to the nature of mind and must actualize that nature in all experiences.

18   The darkness practice retreat is part of the Great Perfection clear light *togyal* practice. Before undergoing the darkness re-

treat, the outer *togyal* practice, which is performed outdoors, must be accomplished. Then the inner *togyal* practice is done in a four-sided hut, with small windows in each direction. The darkness practice follows this, requiring the practitioner to remain in total darkness until the direct perception of clear light arises in the day and night without distinction.

19   The title *ladren* is given, in the Palyul tradition, after a practitioner successfully completes the three year retreat. *Ladren* means junior lama or spiritual teacher. A *ladren* is not necessarily authorized to give empowerments, transmissions or teachings until becoming a *Vajra Acharya* (Tantric Master). A *Vajra Acharya* is one who has achieved meditative realization by successfully completing all the necessary stages of practice.

20   The *Shobul Sutra* is a special food offering prayer, recited by ordained monks and nuns before partaking of the one midday meal. After reciting the prayer, a portion of the food is taken out and offered to the Three Jewels of Refuge. A smaller portion is then taken out and offered to the hungry spirits and the main portion is then eaten.

21   *Sojong* is practiced by ordained monks and nuns on the fifteenth and thirtieth days of the lunar month. Gathering together in the temple, they confess all broken vows and words of honor, and restore and increase all accumulations of virtue and merit.

22   The *dzo* is the result of breeding a *yak* bull and a common cow. The female *dzo* is a common dairy cow of Tibet. A *yak* is the male buffalo of Tibet, having long shaggy hair. These animals are abundant in Tibet, especially in the northeast region.

23   *Kye Dun Rilbu* (Seven Successive Lifetimes-Precious Pill) is a special vase accomplishment ceremony. When a high *bodhisattva* of the Brahmin caste takes seven successive rebirths, after passing from the seventh body, the flesh and bones of that body are considered sacred and potent with the blessing to liberate upon touch and taste. This is used as a precious substance to make countless blessing pills, which are produced, accomplished and consecrated in the vase accomplishment ceremony.

24   A *kanika* stupa has four square sides and a cone-shaped top. Inside the box, the stupa is filled with *tsa-tsa*, small highly con-

secrated stupas. The blessing of the *kanika* stupa is particularly potent. This stupa is commonly found in the region of Palyul in open remote areas.

25 The ritual of blessing the sun's rays is a special *sadhana* from the *Gongdu* revelation of Tertön Sangye Lingpa. This practice condenses all of phenomenal existence into the sun on the thirtieth day of the eleventh lunar month. Then, on the first day of the twelfth month, all of phenomenal existence radiates out with the rays of the rising sun.

26 *Jowo Yidshin Norbu* is a statue made of the likeness of Buddha Shakyamuni and adorned with the crown of the five *Dhyani* Buddhas.

27 Zurchen, Zurchung and his son are the great masters, Zurchen Shakya Jungney, his disciple Zurchung Sherab Tragpa, and his son and disciple, Shakya Yeshe. These three great masters were responsible for the far reaching propagation of the three inner yogas of *Maha, Anu* and *Ati* during their lifetimes.

28 "Like massing clouds, offering goddesses . . .": When the great *Ati Yoga* practitioners pass from the realm of human beings, many primordial wisdom *dakinis* appear to invite and escort them in the transition to the pure realms. When Kunzang Sherab explained that he was receiving this vision, it was a clear sign that he was ready to leave the body.

29 When Kunzang Sherab passed from this world, it was the first Tibetan month, which is the coldest month of the year. The fact that the weather suddenly became warm and spring-like, with sprouts and flowers blooming, was a miraculous sign for that time of year.

CHAPTER SIX:
THE SECOND THRONE HOLDER

1 The eight states of cognition are the consciousness of the sense fields (eye, ear, nose, tongue, body); the consciousness of mental activity; the all-pervasive foundational consciousness and the consciousness of deluded mental activity.

2 The three unmoving states are utilized in the practice of clear light *togyal*. Various postures are assumed, including unmoving body, unmoving visual focus and unmoving mental activity.

3   The three achievements occur when the practitioner is about to realize the results of clear light *togyal* practice. The first achievement is the power over external perceptions and the transformation of all appearances into a pure realm. The second achievement is the power over the inner body and the dissolution of the corporeal body into clear light. The third achievement is the power over the subtle mind and vital air, so that one is able to guide the consciousnesses of other beings to the pure realms. (At this point, one even has the power to guide to the pure realms someone who has accrued the five heinous nonvirtues.)

4   The three gatherings are achieved by great *bodhisattvas* who possess ten powers. One of these ten powers is the power over material objects. Due to this power, the three gatherings are spontaneously actualized. They are: the gathering of many disciples during the daytime; the gathering of primordial wisdom *dakinis* during the night time; and the gathering of wealth during the morning and evening.

5   The three blazings are blazing physical bliss, blazing blessing of speech and blazing realization of the mind.

6   The six ways to plant the seed of liberation in the mind of an aspirant are through seeing, hearing, touching, recollecting, tasting and experiencing. If an aspirant possesses great faith and merit, liberation can actually occur at the moment that the individual comes into contact with a sacred object that has the power of liberating in any of the six ways.

7   The eight worldly concerns are the concern for receiving material offerings or objects, the concern for not receiving material offerings or objects, the concern for happiness, the concern for suffering, the concern for praise, the concern for blame, the concern for fame, and the concern for losing fame. Once entering the path of the dharma, these eight worldly concerns must be eliminated in order for the practice of the dharma to produce pure results.

8   The three trainings are employed in order to maintain daily life discipline as a practicing Buddhist. They are the training in discipline, the training in single-pointed meditative absorption and the training in wisdom.

9   *Sagadawa* is the fourth month of the Tibetan lunar calendar. It was during the first through the fifteenth days of this month

that Buddha Shakyamuni enacted his most powerful miraculous deeds. The fifteenth full moon day of *Sagadawa* is the day of the Buddha's birth, enlightenment and *paranirvana*. It is taught that merit and virtue accumulated during this month is multiplied ten million times over. Likewise, if negative karma is accumulated, the negative results multiply a million times over.

10 The four states of confidence are spontaneously achieved through the practice of the Great Perfection *Ati Yoga*. They are the confidence of recognizing one's own originally pure foundational nature, free from confusion. In this state of confidence, there is no fear of the three lower realms or rebirth there. The second confidence is the pure-awareness state of knowing that *samsara* and *nirvana* are unaccomplished. In this state, there is no longer any hope or fear concerning karmic results. The third confidence is the realization of the empty nature of *nirvana*. The hope to achieve enlightenment ceases to exist. The fourth confidence is the realization that other than one's own pure awareness nature, there is no state of Buddhahood. Here the mind which hopes to achieve Buddhahood and fears lower rebirth is equalized in the view itself.

CHAPTER SEVEN:
THE THIRD THRONE HOLDER

1 *Trekchöd* is one of the two main divisions of practice in the secret oral transmission class of *Ati Yoga*. The practice of *trekchöd* involves actualizing the innermost awareness of one's own primordial wisdom nature, the nature of emptiness.

CHAPTER NINE:
THE FIFTH THRONE HOLDERS

1 Karma Döndam was a renunciate who was always aware of the impermanence of life and all compounded things of this world. It is for this reason that he preferred to keep things around him that reminded him of impermanence. Karma Döndam never prepared for the next day in the same way that others did, because he always assumed that the time of death was uncertain

and he might not be alive to experience tomorrow.

CHAPTER ELEVEN:
THE SEVENTH THRONE HOLDER

1   Other important transmissions which Gyatrul Rinpoche re-
ceived from the second Karma Kuchen Rinpoche Karma Gyur-
med include: Tertön Sangye Lingpa's *Norbu Kor Sum* (Jewel of
Three Cycles); *Tsedrub Nyida Khajor* (Life Accomplishment of
the Conjoined Sun and Moon); Tertön Duddul Lingpa's *Duddul
Chökor* (Dharma Cycle); Tertön Karma Lingpa's *Karling Shi Tro
Kyed Dzog* (Peaceful-Wrathful *Sadhanas* of the Generation and
Completion States); Tertön Mati Ratna's *Mati Sengdong* (Lion-
faced Deity); Tertön Nyang's *Nyang Ter Derdu* (Eight *Herukas*,
Condensed Essence of the *Sugatas*); from Wontrul and Gaje
Tashi Gyatso's lineage, the *Desheg Dupa* (Condensed Essence of
the *Sugatas*) twice; The Life Stories of the Martsang Kagyu
Golden Garland Lineage Holders; The Collected Works of
Lama Boborway; The Collected Works of Kunzang Sherab;
Chagmed Rinpoche's *Richo* (Mountain Retreat Teachings);
naked instructions on *Avalokiteshvara* called, An Ocean Fulfilling the Purpose of Sentient Beings; *Gonpo Solpod* (One Vol-
ume on *Mahakala*); *Kartsi* (White Astrology) from Lama Gon-
sung and Donchog; *Shag Sum Namye* (Astrological Text) from
Dzogchen Dorje Rabten; *Dugor* (Astrological Text); *Yangchar
Khorlo Chagdrid* (Astrological Text); *Jor Drug Nyam Drid* (Experi-
ence-Based Commentary to the Six Unions); Lama Pedma Don-
yod's *Dukhor Dulchen Drimed Od* (The Stainless Light Extensive
Commentary on the *Kalachakra*); Lama Breton's and Kyorawa's
Dukhor Chendrel (*Kalachakra* Word Commentary); Lama Bre-
ton's *Dukhor Chidon* and *Dudon* (General and Condensed Mean-
ing of the *Kalachakra*); Tugsei Lotsawa's Two Volumes of
Teachings; Palyul Lama Pedma Zodpa's *Dowang Rinchen Trengwa*
(*Anu Yoga* Precious Garland Empowerment); *Gyutrul* (*Maha
Yoga*) including the older texts on gathering together empower-
ment materials; *Jangter Gongpa Zang Thal* (The Northern Treasure
Penetrating Enlightened Mind); *Shinje* (Wrathful *Manjusri*); *Keng
Kong* (*Heruka*); *Ta Nag* (Black *Hayagriva*); Bari Tertön's *Seng
Dong* (Lion-faced Deity) and *Gonpo Tsög Dag* (*Mahakala* Owner

of Life); Lhatsei Lama Pedma Chinpa's *Kagyur* transmissions; Terton Jatson Nyingpo's revelations from Yeshe Paljor; *Nam Jom Tro Kar Nag* (The Wrathful Black and White *Dorje Nam Par Jompa*); from Lama Lhundrub *Wangchog Dorje Trengwa* (the empowerment text called, A Vajra Garland); *Drubje Jenang* (Drubje's Transference of Power); and *Dra Kalapa* (Sanskrit Grammar).

2 The transmissions which Gyatrul Rinpoche received from Jamgon Kongtrol Lodrö Thaye Rinpoche include: *Shantong Umai Ta Drid* (*Madhayamika* Text on Emptiness); *Tag Nyi Chidon Tsigdul* (A Tantric Text on the General Explanation and Word Commentary on the Two Examinations); *Zabmo Nangdon* (Profound Inner Meaning); The Collected Works of Karmapa Rangjung Dorje; *Marlug Kyedor* (Marpa's tradition of Kyepa Dorje); *Gur Rigdu Chö Drug* (Six Condensed Works on *Mahakala*); *Zablam Nying Khu* (The Blessing Which Fully Liberates); *Nyingthig Yab Shi* (Four Volumes on *Nyingthig Dzogchen*); *Shinje Chag Dra Chag Dig* (Wrathful *Manjusri*-Iron Scorpion); *Jang Ter Yong Dzog* (All the Northern Treasures); *Nga Ri Kagyed* (Nagari's Eight *Herukas*); *Rigzin Yongdu* (Collection of *Vidyadharas*).

3 The *Dam Ngag Rinpoche Dzöd* (Precious Treasury of Essential Instructions) is the condensed essence of the innermost instruction of the Eight Great Chariots of the Doctrine: the Eight Great Chariots being the first teachers to bring the different lineages to Tibet. They are the three great teachers of the Nyingmapa School, the great teachers of the Gelugpa School, Nagtso Lotsawa, Tsultrim Gyalwa and his disciples Ngog Lotsawa Loden Sherab, Kudon Tsundru Yongtrung, Dromden Gyalwei Jungney and Je Tsongkapa. The founders and great teachers of the Sakya School, Drogmed Lotsawa Shakya Yeshe, Kunga Nyingpo, Tragpa Gyaltsen and Sakya Pandita. The founders and great teachers of the Kagyu School, Marpa Lotsawa, Jetsun Milarepa, Rechungpa and Dragpo Lhaje; Khedrub Chungpo Naljor and Drubchen Thang-thong Gyalpo of the Shangpa Kagyu School; Padampa Sangye, Kyo Shakya Yeshe and Yarlung Marpa Serlo of the Shichedpa School; Kunkhen Dolpopa and Jetsun Drogon of the Dorje Naljor School and Drubchen Oryenpa and Kunkhen Rangjung of the Dorje Nyendrub School.

4 The transmissions which Gyatrul Rinpoche received from Jamyang Khentsey Wangpo include: *Lojong Don Dun* (Seven-Fold Mind Training); *She Tring* (Advice to a Spiritual Friend); *Uma*

Rinchen Trengwa (Precious Garland of the Middle Way); The
Empowerment and Transmission of Thirty Mandalas (from the
earlier *kama* lineage); *Sang Nying Trelwa Gong Gyen* (The Commentary to the Secret Essence called An Ornament of the Enlightened Mind); *Gewa Sum Gyi Don Drid* (Longchenpa's teaching
on The Meaning of the Three Virtues); *Gyutrul Dra Drid* (Teaching on the Illusory Manifestations); *Zab Gya Gyud Chöd* (*Sadhana*
on the Profound Expansive *Tantra*); *Konchog Drelwa* (Rangzom's
Commentary to the Secret Essence); *Chödrag Chidon* (Mindroling
Chödrag's General Meaning); Getsei Panchen's *Sang Nying Legshed Roltso* (Commentary to the Secret Essence called an Ocean
of Eloquent Speech); Jonang's *Drid Gya* (One Hundred Commentaries), these were received in full detail over an extended
period of time; *Jigling Nam Thar* (Jigmed Lingpa's Life Story);
Khentsey Pod Gu (Nine Volumes of Khentsey's Collected Works)
including all empowerments, transmissions and teachings; *Jampal Yang Chan Kor-Rig Tad* (*Manjusri* and Saraswati Cycle-Be-
stowing Wisdom); *Yig Cha Nyingpai Lungchey* (Transmissions of
Older Texts); *Minling Dorsem* (Mindroling Terchen's *Vajrasattva*); *Thug Chen Chöwang; Lama Sangdu* (Guru Chöwang's
Avalokiteshvara and Lama Sangdu's *Avalokiteshvara*); *Chöwang
Phurba* (Guru Chöwang's *Vajrakilaya*); *Trengpo Drol Thig* (Trengpo's Collected Works); *Chögling Thugdrub Namnyi* (Chögyur
Lingpa's Two-fold Mind Accomplishment). After Gyatrul Rinpoche received these transmissions, he held Jamyang Khentsey
Wangpo as his root guru.

From Serthar Washul Lama Sonam Namgyal he received:
Dom Sum Nam Nye Gyi Drelchen (Extensive Commentary of the
Certainty of the Three Vows); Buborwai's *Chagchen Men-ngag
Gyatso* (Ocean of Essential Instruction on the *Mahamudra*);
Kadampai Thegpa Chiching Gyi Drelwa (Kadampa Desheg's Com-
mentary on the General Understanding of the Vehicles); *Gyutrul
Dra Drid* (Illusory Manifestation Commentary); *Jam Chö Kor*
(*Arya Maitreya's* Collected Works); *Lojong Gyatsa* (One Hun-
dred Fold Mind Training); *Sang Nying Yung Tig* (Commentary
to the Secret Essence by Yuldon); *Men Lung Pai Tig* (Commentary to the Secret Essence by Drolchen); *Gog Bub* (Foundation Explanation of the Secret Essence).

From Dzogchen Kongtsa Wonpo Dorje Rabten he received:
Sang Nying Drelwa Par Gab Menkha Balgyi Chen (Commentary

to the Secret Essence by Gegpai Dorje called *Par Gab* and a Commentary to *Par Gab* by Namkha Bal); *Chög Chu Munsel* (Clarifying Darkness in the Ten Directions); *Minling Thug Chen Kyed Dzog Nam Shed* (Commentary to Mindroling's *Avalokiteshvara's* Generation and Completion Stages).

From Gemang Solpon Pedma he received: *Jowo Chö Chung Gyatsa* (One Hundred Short Teachings of Jowo Atisha); *Kamalashila's Gom Rim* (Kamalashila's Stages of Meditation); *Kama Rong Phur* (Rong Zam's *Vajrakilaya* from the *kama*); *Rog Phur* (Rog's *Vajrakilaya* from the *kama*); *Bum Nag* (*Vajrakilaya* from the *kama*); *Kha Thun* (*Manjusri*-Kha Thun); *Dorje Zampa* (Vajra Bridge); *Kadam Sung Dor* (Teachings of the Kadampa Tradition); *Chig Lab Ringpo* (Teachings of the Kadampa Tradition); *Dudtsi Chu Gyur* (Continual Flow of Nectar); *Legshed Kundu* (Condensation of Eloquent Speech); *Khentsey Pod Gu* (Nine Volumes of Khentsey's Collected works); *Dzabhir Lung Drid* (Dzabhir's Teachings on Vital Air); Gendun Gyatso's *Tsan Jod Trig* (The First Dalai Lama's Commentary on Praising the Names of *Manjusri*) *Mitra Drid Drug* (Six Commentaries of Mitra); *Kunkhyen Sung Thor Kor* (Longchenpa's Expositions in Brief).

From Dzonser Nyari Lama Kunga Jamyang he received: *Pe Chö Rinpung Tam Gyun* (Rinpung's Accounts of the Past); *Menngag Rinpung* (Rinpung's Essential Instructions); *Trophu Men-ngag Gyatsa* (Trophu's One Hundred Essential Instructions); *Jonang Dang Shangpai Lam Rin* (Graduated Path of Jonang and Shangpa); *Dagpoi Thar Gyan* (Dagpo Rinpoche's Ornament of Liberation); *Sa Phur* (Sakyapa's *Vajrakilaya*); *Be Bum Ngon Moi Drelwa* (Green Be Bum's Commentary); *Drigung Gong Chig* (Drigung Kargyu's One Enlightened Mind); *Gyathong Chöd Pod* (Gyathong's Volume on Exorcism); *Lam Dre Dra Don* (Sakyapa's Path and Fruition); *Lam Dre Pod Ser Chö Tsan Shi* (Sakyapa's Four Volumes on the Path and Fruition); *Lam Dre Pod Mar Chö Tsan Don Nga* (Sakyapa's Seventy-five Volumes on the Path and Fruition); *Lam Kor Chi Ma Gyad* (Eight Later Divisions of the Path); *Morchen Nang Gyud* (Morchen's *Tantra* on Perception); Khentsey's *Sung Gur* (Khentsey Rinpoche's Dharma Songs); *Ka Bum Pod Nyi* (Two Volumes of Khentsey Rinpoche's Collected Works).

5 The six traditional ornaments are usually sculpted behind the main images in a large temple. They are the elephant, snow lion, black antelope, human champion, a mythological monster

fish and the garuda.

6   The thirty great mandalas are uniquely constructed by using finely ground substances. The best substances used are gold, silver and precious jewels. Other substances usually used are finely ground grain, stone or sand. Colors are applied to the powder, depending on the color scheme of each individual mandala.

7   The offering of fertile fields and the yield of crops to monks and monasteries was commonplace in Tibet. Fully-ordained monks are not allowed to work in the fields, so the crops that laymen grew would often be offered, as well as the proceeds from those crops.

CHAPTER TWELVE:
THE EIGHTH THRONE HOLDER

1   *Torma* offerings to the hungry spirits are traditionally made in the morning by offering water blessed with special pills. The practitioner imagines that this small offering increases to fulfill all the desires and needs of countless wandering hungry spirits. Then, through the power of single-pointed concentration, the spirits are invoked and they come to partake of the offerings, thereby satisfying themselves. The *sang* smoke offering is first made to all the objects of refuge, then to the local and hungry spirits, as well as the beings who are owed unpaid karmic debts from past lifetimes.

2   *Tsa-tsa* and *mani* stones are both traditional offerings made in great quantities in Tibet. *Tsa-tsa* are small impressions of stupas made out of clay which also contain dharma medicine, relics and/or mantras as consecration materials. *Mani* stones are large flat stones which have the mantra *Om Mani Pedme Hung* hand carved on them. The *tsa-tsa* and *mani* stones are usually piled together in places where people can circumambulate to acquire merit and virtue.

3   *Yarney* is the traditional rainy season retreat carried out in monastic institutions. Each rainy season the weather becomes warm and humid, so that the insect population flourishes. Since the season usually lasts for three months (in Asia), ordained monks and nuns take a vow to remain in the confines of the

monastic compound to avoid killing insects and thus breaking their vows. In addition, it is a time that was very bad for the health of the body. The *yarney* retreat was practiced annually at the Palyul monastery in Tibet and the tradition continues on at Namdroling monastery in South India.

4   Dharma medicine pills increasing and rolling down the mandala cord towards Do-ngag Chökyi Nyima refers to the accomplishment ceremony which is performed by constructing a mandala. All the lamas and practitioners visualize themselves as the deity and the mandala as the assembly of deities in the space in front. The *Vajra Acharya* presiding over the ceremony (in this case Do-ngag Chökyi Nyima) holds a vajra to his heart, which is wrapped by a cord, connected to the central vase within the mandala. This symbolizes the radiation of light between self-generation and the generation in front. During this visualization, some of the blessed pills inside of the mandala spontaneously rolled down the cord to the vajra at Do-ngag Chökyi Nyima's heart. This is a true sign of accomplishment.

5   The flesh and blood of the enemy of the doctrine suddenly appearing on his table, refers to extraordinary *Vajrayana* practice that is performed to benefit beings in the most expedient way. However, such a practice must be performed by one who has full power beyond the trace of any doubt. The practice referred to here is called *dralwa* which is the liberation of the consciousness of a negative entity or harmful being. There are ten reasons for performing a *dralwa*, which must be complete before the wrathful activity is activated. If negative beings are allowed to continue accumulating extremely negative karma in these ten ways, then the immediate next rebirth is taken in the lowest hell realms. A fully-qualified practitioner can see this and has the power to consciously guide and liberate the consciousness to higher realms and to realize Buddhahood. The practice is an act of intense compassion, with profound immediate results. The sign of the effective accomplishment of *dralwa* during these ceremonies was clear when the corpse of the enemy suddenly and miraculously appeared on his table.

CHAPTER THIRTEEN:
THE NINTH THRONE HOLDER

1   From the time that the first Drubwang Pedma Norbu made this prophecy, three hundred years passed before the juniper tree next to his residence bore a single berry.

CHAPTER FOURTEEN:
THE TENTH THRONE HOLDER

1   The lower activity is the part of the *sadhana* practice which is performed by a qualified practitioner to reverse and eliminate all obstructing forces and negative entities through engaging in wrathful activity. This display of miraculous activity is the extreme expression of compassion and can only be performed effectively by a highly qualified adept.

CHAPTER FIFTEEN:
THE ELEVENTH THRONE HOLDER

1   During the time of taking ordination, there must be at least five previously ordained *gelongs* (monks) present and ideally ten. The person receiving vows must then request the senior most high ranking monk to be the *khenpo* (abbott). The *khenpo* blesses all the new articles that will belong to the monk, such as the robes, begging bowl and so forth. Then the *khenpo* asks questions of the vow recipient concerning the pure maintenance of the vows. The *khenpo* appoints a second monk, called the *lelob* (action teacher), to recite all the necessary prayers and recitations three times. After this, the vows are fully received. Then, a third monk, the *sangtön* (secret teacher) asks very personal questions of the vow recipient. A fourth monk states the exact year, month, day and time that the vows have been received. A fifth monk is the helper, who assists the new vow recipient during the ceremony. The additional monks present fulfill the auspicious and correct number of monks present during an ordination ceremony.

2   The first five fortunate disciples originated twenty-eight years

after Lord Buddha Shakyamuni passed into *paranirvana.* At that
time, the god, Dragden Chögkyong; the *naga*, Jogpo; the demi-
god, Kardadong; the demon, Lodrö Tabden; and the human,
Vidyadhara Drimed Tragpa; were all in deep meditative absorption in their respective places. Simultaneously they arose
from meditation, realizing that the world where Buddha had
come and taught would fall once again into turmoil. Miraculously (through their powers) they all gathered together at Sri
Lanka and congregated at the peak of the great Namchag Barwa mountain. Exchanging twenty-three words of sorrow over
the absence of the enlightened teacher who illuminates the
darkness in the troubled minds of sentient beings, they lament-
ed and offered profoundly deep prayers. Because of the power
and force of their united prayers, *Vajrapani,* the owner of the
secret vehicle, appeared before them. *Vajrapani* transmitted
the Dharma Wheel of the *Vajrayana* Doctrine, which Buddha
had taught in Akanishtha (the highest pure realm) to these first
five disciples and then to countless *Vidyadharas.* This was the
very first time that the *Vajrayana* teachings were given in this
world. When Khenpo Khentsey Lodrö transmitted his newly
written commentaries on the *Anu Yoga* teachings to this group
of five fortunate disciples, it was also the very first time, creating an auspicious coincidence, according to *Vajrayana.*

3 These sacred tongue-woven blessing cords are extremely rare
and can be made only by a highly accomplished lama. The
lama, using only his tongue, creates an extremely intricate knot,
woven in a single thread. The precious cords made by the third
Pedma Norbu Rinpoche are especially intricate and astonishing
to see. For reasons that are unknown, the tongue-woven cords
have not been made by him since 1958.

4 The three secrets refer to the inherent primordial wisdom
nature of secret body, speech and mind. Since only an enlightened being can perceive this nature, and sentient beings can-
not, because of their ignorance, the term secret is used.

CHAPTER SIXTEEN:
OTHER IMPORTANT PALYUL LAMAS

1   The Kunzang Khorlo (Wheel of Praise) that Chögtrul Rinpoche composed is an extremely sophisticated poetic work of art. The composer traditionally uses his own spiritual teacher as the subject of praise. The name of the teacher is written so that it appears in a circular pattern wherever one reads.

CHAPTER SEVENTEEN:
CONCLUSION

1   This prayer in the original Tibetan is poetically composed as a prayer to the founder of this tradition, the great Vidyadhara Kunzang Sherab. Kunzang means complete excellence which is also the name of the primordial Buddha. Sherab means wisdom.

Postscript

Since the translation of *A Garland of Immortal Wish-fulfilling Trees* was completed in the fall of 1986, many important events have taken place increasing the scope of the Palyul lineage throughout the world. As these events have a profound impact on the Nyingma school in particular, and the propagation of the dharma in general, a brief postscript is included.

The activities of His Holiness the Third Drubwang Pedma Norbu Rinpoche have increased bringing waves of benefit to all beings. In March of 1986, the first group of scholars trained under His Holiness' guidance graduated from the largest Nyingma scholastic college in the world at Palyul Namdroling monastery in South India. Shortly before the commencement, several of the monks were tested in debate by His Holiness the Dalai Lama.

The following May, His Holiness Pedma Norbu Rinpoche made his second trip to Tibet since leaving in 1960. Accompanied by the Venerable Gyatrul Rinpoche and an entourage of 20 monks, His Holiness visited the provinces of Ü-tsam, Golok and Kham. Ordaining hundreds of monks, consecrating stupas, and bestowing empowerments on thousands wherever he visited, His Holiness also visited the principal Buddhist pilgrimage points in mainland China. After eight months in Tibet, in January 1988, His Holiness traveled to Bhutan to give the *Nam Chö* empowerments of Tertön Migyur Dorje to more than seven thousand people.

In May of 1988, His Holiness will begin his second worldwide tour. With an entourage of over 15 monks, including dancers, musicians and chanters, His Holiness will visit Taiwan, the United States and Canada. During this trip, His Holiness will give the complete *Kama, Rinchen Ter Dzöd, Longchen Nyingthig* and *Zab Mo Yangthig.* All these teachings will be accompanied by the appropriate dances of the Three Roots to firmly establish the blessings of the Buddha

Dharma and harmonize the land. This is the first time the dances
have been done in America. In Taiwan, His Holiness will preside
over the cremation of the Venerable Dzongnang Rinpoche, Jampal
Lodro, who passed away suddenly in August of 1987 in Hong
Kong.

Then, arriving in the United States in June, His Holiness will
begin a series of three major cycles of teachings. At Tashi Chöling,
the retreat center for Pacific Yeshe Nyingpo in Ashland, Oregon,
which is under the guidance of the Venerable Gyatrul Rinpoche,
His Holiness will bestow the complete Nyingma *Kama* as well as
the *lung* for *Nam Chö*. Traveling to Canada, he will give the *Longchen
Nyingthig* and *Zab Mo Yangthig* of Longchen Rabjampa at Orgyan
Osal Chö Dang in Ontario.

In August, His Holiness will arrive at the seat of the Palyul lineage
in the West, Kunzang Odsal Palyul Changchub Chöling. Here His
Holiness will bestow the entire *Rinchen Ter Dzöd* (Precious *Terma*
Treasury) for the first time in the West.

Kunzang Odsal Palyul Changchub Chöling is directed by Tulku
Ahkön Norbu Lhamo, Catharine Burroughs. In April of 1987, His
Holiness recognized her as the incarnation of Genyenma Ahkön
Lhamo, the sister of Vidyadhara Kunzang Sherab and also a direct
student of Tertön Migyur Dorje. In her lifetime, the first Ahkön
Lhamo was recognized as a primordial wisdom *dakini* whose
prayers and aspirations were instrumental in establishing the first
Palyul monastery. At the time of her cremation, the *kapala* flew
from the funeral pyre three kilometers, landing at the throne of her
brother Kunzang Sherab. Embossed with the syllable *Ah*, it was one of
the most treasured relics at the monastery used only during great
accomplishment ceremonies. It is remarkable that as a young boy,
His Holiness had made special prayers to find the incarnation of
Ahkön Lhamo who is still remembered throughout the Palyul
monasteries in Tibet.

Besides giving teachings, His Holiness will also ordain a number
of students at Kunzang Odsal Palyul Changchub Chöling, as well as
consecrate the site of nine stupas and a temple.

As the precious doctrine of Lord Buddha takes root in the
western world, we must acknowledge the kindness and the prophecies of Guru Padmasambhava as they unfold in the second half
of this century.

In this degenerate time, when negative forces, incurable disease and dangerous armies surround us, while perverted prayers are increasing, through the purity of the doctrine and the kindness of those whose breath upholds it, may all beings be blessed by the truth of the Three Precious Jewels and the Three True Roots. Through the increase of this lineage and the miraculous activities of its holders may the message of liberation spread like the morning sun, illuminating and upholding the path of liberation for all beings everywhere!

April, 1988
Poolesville, Maryland